ੴ ਸਤਿਨਾਮੁ ਸ੍ਰੀ ਵਾਹਿਗੁਰੂ

Dedicated to the Children of the Aquarian Age

ੴ ਸਤਿਨਾਮੁ ਸ੍ਰੀ ਵਾਹਿਗੁਰੂ

Ek Ong Kar Sat Nam Siri Wha-he Guru
THERE IS BUT ONE GOD, TRUTH IS HIS NAME,
GREAT IS HIS INDESCRIBABLE WISDOM.

DESIGN:Armando Busick, Parmatma Singh Khalsa
COVER ART: Seva Singh Khalsa
COVER DESIGN: Aradhana Singh Khalsa
TEXT ILLUSTRATION: Linda Gale, Roger Rudolph
EDITORS: Steve Gilbar, Parmatma Singh Khalsa

ISBN 0-9655523-0-6 (previously ISBN 0-913852-01-5)

First Printing — June 1972: 3,000
Second Printing —March 1973: 5,000
Third Printing— November 1996: 3,000

For other works published by Yogi Ji Press write or fax us.
For more information on Sikh Dharma contact 3HO, 1620
Preuss Rd., Los Angeles, CA 90035. (310) 273-9422.
For a catalog of natural products and books containing the
teachings of Yogi Bhajan:
The Ancient Healing Ways Catalog
Rt 3 Box 259, Espanola NM 87532
U.S. (800)359-2940 Intrntl. (505)747-2860

PUBLISHED AND DISTRIBUTED BY

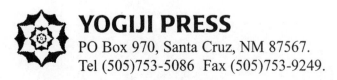

YOGIJI PRESS
PO Box 970, Santa Cruz, NM 87567.
Tel (505)753-5086 Fax (505)753-9249.

CONTENTS

PART III — KARTARPUR

ONG NAMO GURU DEV NAMO
Salutations to the Creator, to the Divine Teacher salutations.

INTRODUCTION
by Yogi Bhajan

Throughout the cycle of time, the Ages change—like the change from dawn to dusk. Sometimes dharma rules and righteousness prevails. Man then walks with the consciousness of Truth; he lives in the bounty of beauty and the flow of love. The individual soul is in communion with the Supreme Soul. This Age of Truth changes when Man forgets the Creator, the cause of every effect, and fails to dedicate his actions to Him. The individual ego becomes confined in selfish activity. The G-O-D (G for Generating principle; O for Organizing principle; and D for Destroying principle) is forgotten and the gap which grows between Man and his own higher consciousness brings him pain and misery. Individual man becomes so limited that he finds it difficult to sustain himself.

Today we live in such a chaotic age—Kali Yug. Man wants to seek God, to realize Him in his higher consciousness. He searches for methods and techniques to break down the boundaries which separate him from God and reactivate the flow of consciousness by merging into the Supreme Consciousness of the Cosmos. In this Age spiritual teachers abound, but many, unfortunately, instead of guiding Man to freedom, are so entrapped in their own "spiritual egos" that they act as traps, like a web for the fly, where a man is sucked dry.

In times like these, 500 years ago, in the skies of India there were dark, dark clouds. Righteousness was nowhere to be found. Ego and selfishness were eating humanity, rulers were massacring the innocent, and the earth was soaked with blood. The cries of the poor and the innocent reached the Creator, and by the mercy of His Supreme Consciousness, He manifested through a very pure and humble channel in the form of Guru Nanak.

Nanak was a man of consciousness and universal awareness. His Guru was the Shabad (Word) and with the practice of the Word and the Nam (Holy Name of God) he praised the Lord, singing to Him in the ecstatic rhythm and melody of that Divine flow which soothed embittered minds and gave happiness and contentment to men. He traveled throughout the East, showing the so-called holy men of his time the traps of maya, exposing their spiritual egos and giving them the message of brotherhood and God-consciousness. His practical approach is a clear demonstration of the continuous manifestation of God's light, leading to the infinite and total supremacy of the higher consciousness which is beyond all outward robes and rituals.

The powerful radiance of compassion and Truth shining through his words clearly showed humanity that only by creating the holy vibration or Nam in ecstasy, by preparing the physical body to vibrate the Name of God, and by tuning the mind to beam this Name, could the individual consciousness merge into the Supreme Universal Consciousness.

Guru Nanak served humanity by openly teaching this technique of awareness in order to bring men out from the pit of hell into which they had been dragged by the blind, ritualistic, self-centered, spiritual egotists of that dark age. He gave men freedom of the Spirit and took away the domination of these "middle men." Humanity had committed the error time and again of worshipping the man rather than the Truth he represents. Guru Nanak taught that it is the God who prevails through the man, and the man—however great he may be—is only the channel, the instrument for the flow of the Divine Wisdom. Men are meant to praise God, and to teach others to do so, not to become objects of worship themselves. Thus, Guru Nanak re-established righteousness and the path to glory in his own time. He made mankind understand the basic law of life: *"Nanak Nam Chardi kala, tere bhane sarbat ka bhala."*—Keep up and wish good to all.

He explained to people in practical ways the ecstasy of the Nam and gave them the technical know-how to reach that higher stage of consciousness themselves. Over and above all this, he sang *"Nam kumari Nanaka charhi rahe dinrat."* —Nanak is intoxicated, oh Lord, with thy Holy Name all day and night.

Guru Nanak lived in the Will of his Creator, and showed people that the highest stage of awareness for a man or woman is to live fulfilled as a man or woman; then the grace of God will prevail. Man should not forget that he has been created by the Creator, and the Creator created as He chose best. Therefore, it is best for us to live as we have been created. He also reminded Man that the breath of life comes to him from the infinite source of energy, which is undying and bountiful—Pavan Guru. All these things he made Man think and feel. He brought this awareness to prepare humanity for the coming change of time and the stars.

In the cycle of time, now dawns the Age of Aquarius, where Uranus shall be the ruling star and Man shall REALIZE and KNOW before believing, rather than believe and accept before knowing. The present Piscean Age with its narrow reliance on blind faith and tradition must now give way to the Golden Age of self-realization through practical experience. The teacher for this glorious age of the brotherhood of man, the humble instrument of the Lord who brought the practical message of how each man can relate to the flow of the God-consciousness within himself, is Sat Guru Nanak. Through his teachings and the example of his life, today's children of the Aquarian Age can find that guidance, that inspiration, and that courage to meet the test of the times and ever walk on the path of righteousness in the light of the Truth.

It has been the humble effort of this individual, inspired by the grace of God in a merciful moment of bliss, to act to have this work published for the general knowledge of all seekers of Truth. It is a timeless message for today brought to this earth 500 years ago. May all who read it relate to it with their higher consciousness and experience that Knowledge of Oneness in the One Truth that Guru Nanak taught then and is teaching even now. Sat Nam.

May 4, 1972

YOGI BHAJAN

FOREWORD

I have come to the world in search of Truth—Guru Nanak

Guru Nanak was born in 1469 A.D. at Talwandi, a small village forty miles from Lahore, now in Pakistan. In his childhood he preferred the company of wandering holy men to that of his schoolmates. He worked at several professions, married and was the father of two sons.

Still in his twenties, he left his family and took to the road with two companions: Bala, a Hindu, and Mardana, a Muslim. His travels took him as far as Assam in the East, Ceylon in the South, Mecca in the West and Tibet in the North. On these trips he came into contact with many different beings—rich, poor, prominent, common, Sufis, yogis, lamas, cannibals, magicians and the first Moghul Emperor, Babar. To all of them he brought his message of Truth: to love Man and God.

During the last fifteen years of his life Guru Nanak settled in the town of Kartarpur where he continued to teach. The low consciousness in the political, social, economic and religious institutions of his times paralleled that of today. He was an outspoken critic of these conditions and taught practical ways for Man to liberate himself from them. Ethics and morality were the very foundation of Guru Nanak's teachings. Spiritual evolution was not possible without righteous living. For Nanak there was no difference between the every day life and the spiritual life. At Kartarpur he worked as a farmer and supplied free food from a common kitchen, where all, regardless of caste or religion, were fed from the same platform.

Guru Nanak strove to purify the religious institutions of his time. He sacrificed his eldest son, Baba Siri Chand, to this end by ordaining him as head of a group of ascetic yogis. At that time many yogis and other "holy men" were obsessed with having occult powers and were harassing the ordinary householder. Baba Siri Chand went around the country preaching the Name of God to the egocentric yogis and brought them back on the path of love and supreme consciousness.

Those who gathered around Guru Nanak were known in the Punjabi language as "sikhs"—disciples of the Guru, both of Guru Nanak and of the Universal Guru, whose wisdom and teachings Nanak humbly manifested. "The Guru makes a devotee conscious of his higher needs and sets him on the path of love, service and devotion," said Nanak.

Guru Nanak died at Kartarpur in 1539 A.D. and one of his disciples, Angad, received the Guruship. In all, there were eleven Gurus in what became the Sikh Dharma—ten men and a holy book, the Guru Granth Sahib, which contains the sacred teachings of Guru Nanak and others.

Guru Nanak is one of the great spiritual teachers to have walked upon the earth. We are privileged to have published this edition of his life and teachings through the sponsorship of Yogi Bhajan, who has brought the Guru's message to the United States.

8

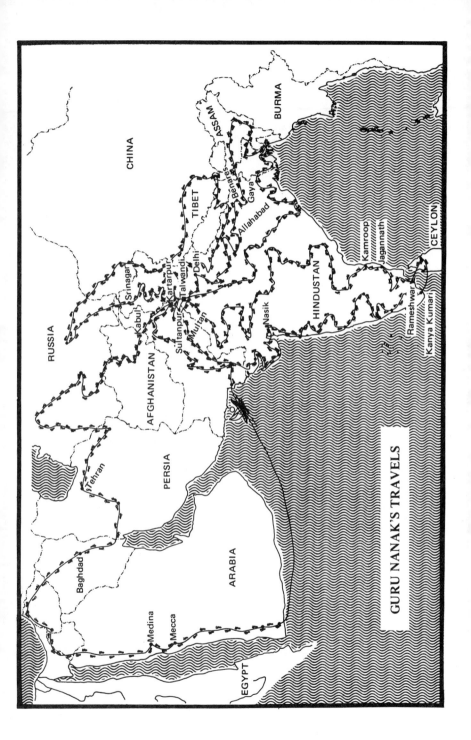

GURU NANAK'S TRAVELS

RUSSIA

CHINA

ASSAM

BURMA

TIBET

Benares

Gaya

Allahabad

Srinagar

Kabul

Kartarpur

Talwandi

Delhi

Sultanpur

Multan

Nasik

HINDUSTAN

Kamroop

Jagannath

CEYLON

Rameshwar

Kanya Kumari

AFGHANISTAN

Tehran

PERSIA

Baghdad

ARABIA

Medina

Mecca

EGYPT

9

PROLOGUE

When Guru Nanak came into this world it was said he laughed like an adult.

It was said that the wise of the community could hear celestial music.

The family astrologer, on seeing the baby, greeted him with joined palms declaring that he would sit under a royal canopy, that he would be worshipped by Hindus and Muslims alike, that even the inanimate objects of nature would utter his name with reverence.

PART I

HOME AND FAMILY

Guru Nanak's mother, Matta Tripat, nursed him with loving care and soon discovered that he was not like other babies. He never cried for his mother as other babies did, but lay calmly in his cradle gazing upward with his deep luminous eyes. In due time he learned to walk and to talk, but he never played like other children of his age. He would sit as if lost in contemplation. He would give the other children his toys and persuade his mother to feed them milk and cookies, wanting nothing for himself.

Mehta Kalu, Guru Nanak's father, was a high ranking civil servant, much esteemed in his community. He was also a landowner, and had a large herd of cattle. Nanak had an older sister, Bibi Nanki, after whom he was named.

When he was nine years old, his father enrolled him in the small school run by the village Pandit—a learned man.

The Pandit began Nanak's first lesson by writing out a few letters on a slate and asking the boy to repeat each letter after him. Nanak learned the alphabet in no time as though he had known it already. He then turned to his teacher and asked,

"What are these letters meant for?"

"Two or three letters make a word, words makes sentences," replied the Pandit, "and thus transmit knowledge and wisdom from age to age."

Nanak took the slate and sat aside lost in thought, joined the letters and formed words. The teacher turned to him and saw he was sitting quietly, motionless, eyes fixed on the slate as though wholly absorbed in it.

"Why are you sitting as if struck dumb?" asked the Pandit with impatience.

"I have put the letters together and formed a word," replied the boy.

"What is it?" asked the Pandit.

"I have made HIM," said the boy.

"My son, what are you trying to read into these simple symbols?" asked the Pandit on receiving this unexpected reply.

"He who has created this Universe," said Nanak. "He is the One.

He is the Lord of all."

"What more is passing through your little mind?" asked the Pandit with an indulgent smile.

"Thus," said Nanak with conviction, "all learning is in vain, except to know Him and to serve Him."

The Pandit was astonished at the boy's precociousness. "What do you know about Him?" he asked.

"This, that to love Him is the end of knowledge and to forget Him is to forget the truth, even though one may carry a cartload of books," said Nanak.

The boy seemed to have passed into a state of ecstasy and spoke as if from some far away height. The Pandit was bewildered but wanted to test him and said, "God, of whom you speak, what is He and where is He?"

"This creation is His," said Nanak, "and He is everywhere."

"Why can't we feel Him and see Him?" saked the Pandit.

A flickering smile passed over Nanak's lips as he answered, "Do the blind see the sun?"

"No," said the Pandit.

"Are we not blind?" asked Nanak. "Blind to all else, but sense-objects. He is beyond all senses and it is only when the darkness of the senses is removed that He can be seen. His love pervades all things."

"If His love is in all things, why is there sorrow and suffering?" asked the Pandit.

"The answer is simple. You could have found it if you had searched your heart. When we act against the law of love, we chain ourselves to the wheel of cause and effect," said Nanak.

"You mean we create Karma?" asked the Pandit.

"Yes," said Nanak.

"It has been said by wise ones that with the fire of knowledge the seed of Karma can be permanently destroyed," remarked the Pandit.

"Yes, with realization, but not with book knowledge," said Nanak. "He alone is learned who knows Him."

He then took up each letter of the alphabet and said, "As letters are symbols of speech, so various forms are manifestations of God. He is the Enjoyer of all sense-objects. He is within and without all beings. He who knows that God is all and in all and consequently loses all sense of otherness, he alone escapes from the prison of I-AM-NESS. In selfhood is bondage; in losing the self, freedom."

The Pandit was not only astonished, but convinced that Nanak was an incarnation of God. He humbly bowed before his pupil and took him to his father.

Mehta Kalu was sitting with some friends. He was surprised to see his son and his teacher coming back to him so early. Nanak must have done something wrong and the Pandit was bringing him back to be reprimanded, he thought.

"This son of yours is an Avatar, an incarnation of God, and no ordinary mortal," said the Pandit as he took a seat near Mehta Kalu. "He has come to redeem the victims of Kali Yug, this dark age."

Mehta Kalu smiled in disbelief. He was a worldly man and thought the Pandit was just flattering the boy. He wanted his son to be wise in the ways of the world, to know how to gain riches and power. So he said, "You are paying the boy a great compliment, but I trust you will continue to instruct him."

"Instruct him! How?" exclaimed the Pandit. "He knows all that there is to be known."

"What does he know?" asked Mehta Kalu.

"He knows more than I do," answered the Pandit. "He knows God is One, Infinite without a second. He is the Author of all Creation. He knows that to transgress the law of love is to sin. He knows that I-AM-NESS is the disease and carries its own cure. Tell me what more is there to know?" said the Pandit.

Mehta Kalu looked at the Pandit with disbelieving eyes, but the Pandit rose and prostrated himself at the feet of the Guru and before departing again repeated, "My dear Mehta, I am not a fool. I believe in what I have said, your son has all the characteristics of an Avatar."

THE COBRA KNEW

Like all fathers, Mehta Kalu wanted his son to follow the path which he himself had found profitable. He just could not accept his son's lack of interest in anything which he considered practical. He watched him carefully and soon discovered that he enjoyed caring for animals. He also noticed that he enjoyed being out-of-doors, prefering to spend his days out in the fields sitting under a tree. This gave gave him the idea that he might interest his son in becoming a stock-breeder. The next day he said to him, "You seem to be fond of cows and buffaloes."

"I am;" said the boy, "they can't ask for what they want so I like to give them what they need."

"How do you know what they need?" asked the father.

"Through sympathy and understanding," he replied. "They have, like us, hunger not only of the body but of the soul as well."

Not liking the direction the conversation was taking, Mehta Kalu suddenly suggested, "If you're so fond of animals, why not take out a herd to graze?"

"Nothing would please me more," said Nanak. "Then I could

make sure that they were well fed."

So he began to take a small herd out, the cows and buffaloes following him as if they had always belonged to him. Each evening he would bring them home.

One day while sitting in deep meditation under a banyan tree, unaware of the world around him, his cattle strayed into a neighboring field and feasted on the growing crop. Just as they had almost finished grazing, the owner of the field appeared and saw the result of his labor in ruin. He angrily turned to the boy and screamed, "Wake up, you lazy fool, see what your cattle have done. They've ruined my crop. How am I and my family to live?"

Nanak looked up, his eyes filled with compassion, and said, "Have patience, your field will give you a greater return than ever before."

"You can't deceive me by words," he said. "I'm going to the village chief, Rai Bular. He'll make your father pay the full value of the crop." Shouting and complaining, he ran to the village.

Then the boy, his eyes full of love, gazed upon the ruined field and it smiled back a green and luxuriant crop.

Meanwhile, the owner found Rai Bular and bitterly told him of his loss. "Calm down," the chief said. "I'll send an appraiser with you who will estimate the loss and I'll personally see that you are fully compensated." He gave instructions to the appraiser who, accompanied by the owner, came to the field. They were astonished when they arrived, for the field was lush with a growing crop.

The appraiser began to yell at the owner. "Have you no eyes? Were you blind not to see that your crop was all right?"

The owner could not believe his eyes. He touched the crop with his hands and held his head down and said, "What can I say? A miracle has happened. My eyes did not deceive me. I was in full possession of my senses. I saw what I saw."

The appraiser returned to Rai Bular and told him what had happened. He had heard of Nanak and the episode with his teacher and this confirmed his belief that Nanak was no ordinary boy.

A few days later, Rai Bular saw an astonishing scene himself. He was returning from an adjoining village, when from a distance, he saw Nanak sleeping in a pasture with a cobra raised above him, its hood protecting the boy's head from the scorching sun, while all the cattle sat peacefully around. Thinking that Nanak was bitten or dead, he rushed to the spot. As he reached the boy, the cobra disappeared and Nanak got up and greeted him with a smile. Rai Bular was so moved that he jumped down from his horse, embraced the boy and kissed him. From that day forward, he never failed to support the young Nanak whom he believed to be a messenger of God.

When the story of the grazing of the field reached Mehta Kalu, he decided that he could no longer trust his son with the care of his animals. After a long talk with his wife, he decided to take a firm stand with Nanak and put him in some profession for which he expressed a liking.

"I am old," he told his son, "and may pass away any time. You will have to take my place. Your mother will have to depend on you. You must not waste your time any more, but must do something useful."

"Father, if you're aware that you may soon die, what preparations are you making to attain happiness in the other world?"

His father held his breath; he could not find an answer.

"It's not good to talk of such things," interrupted his mother.

This gave his father a chance to gather his thoughts. He added that there was plenty of time to think of the other world. "We should think of the world in which we live. If you don't do anything in this world, you will be bankrupt and go empty-handed to the other. Now listen, I have a small area of land. Why don't you start farming it?"

"Father, I am always engaged in real farming."

> This body is the field
> The mind is the farmer
> Modesty the irrigating water.
> I plant the seed of the Divine Name
> and with the plow of contentment
> crush the crust of pride into true humility.
> In it the seed of love will prosper.
> Seated in the house of truth
> I watch its progress.
> Father, Greed does not accompany man,
> The world is deluded by it.
> Only a few walk out of delusion and attain truth.

His father refused to pay any attention to his son's words and continued, "If farming doesn't appeal to you, why not open a shop?" The Guru again answered,

> I make this frail body my shop
> I make meditation the container
> I stock it with the true Name
> I trade with the dealers of the true Name
> And thus accumulate the wealth of truth.

17

His father remained unconvinced and pressed him to become a dealer in horses. The Guru answered him again in another parable.

> He is a true dealer in horses
> Who breeds the horses of truth,
> Stores wealth of virtue
> To meet the needs of the way,
> And worries no more,
> Full of unfailing faith
> That in the abode of the Formless
> He shall share its bliss.

Kalu was now in despair, but he persisted in impressing on his son the need of doing something. "If you're not ready to go into business then you had better work for the government. I have some influence and can easily arrange it for you." The Guru replied,

> I serve my Master;
> You too should serve Him
> With your whole heart
> With your passions subdued,
> Perform action with His Name in your heart:
> When He looks on you with favor
> Your face will shine with splendor,
> You shall be greatly blessed.

Having said this, he went into deep meditation.

THE SACRED THREAD

Years passed and the Guru reached the age when according to the custom of his family, he was to be invested with the sacred thread, an important religious and caste ritual. The day fixed by the family priest, Harydal, as auspicious for the ceremony arrived. Elaborate preparations had been made for its performance. Family relations and friends from near and far had been invited and, as was the custom, a great feast had been arranged. Harydal was in great form. He had the courtyard floor replastered. On a raised platform he spread a woolen carpet, drew a circle around it, and then took his seat with all the implements of the ceremony around him.

He then asked Mehta Kalu to bring his son for whom a seat was provided facing the priest. Nanak took his seat, his eyes sparkling with amusement. There was something about his gentle face which attracted the eyes of all the guests.

Harydal began invoking the blessings of the stars by chanting in Sanskrit, then blessed the boy by reciting Vedic mantras and finally blessed the sacred thread itself. He was about to place it around Nanak's neck, when the boy stopped him.

"What is this cotton thread?" he asked. "Why is it worn? And what advantage does it give the wearer?"

"This thread is a symbol of high lineage and spiritual inheritance," replied Harydal.

"How is this thread made?" asked Nanak. "Who makes it? Doesn't it decay? How does it absorb spiritual power?"

Harydal was confused, but answered, "It is made out of pure cotton. A Brahmin makes it and endows it with the power of mantra. When it decays, it is replaced by a new one."

"Why, may I ask, are goats killed and feasts given?" asked the Guru.

"Your father and his guests are of a caste for which it is lawful to eat meat," replied the priest.

The Guru raised his large luminous eyes and said,

> What strange ceremony is this?
> The Brahmin spins a thread out of cotton
> And twists it into shape.
> When it decays, a new one takes its place.
> If the thread had any virtue
> It would not decay or break.
> They kill goats without mercy
> And prepare a feast
> And guests clamor for more and more.

Having spoken, the Guru rose from his seat and, turning to the assembled guests, quietly said,

> My elders, worthy of all respect,
> Is it not strange
> That he who performs the ceremony
> And claims to foretell the future
> Charges a fee for the performance?
> He places no control on his senses
> Nor protects his beard from the spit of greed.
> He puts no restraint on his eyes or tongue,
> On his hands and feet.
> In all actions, he is unrestrained
> And yet he puts a twisted thread
> Round the neck of another.
> See this strange phenomenon—
> The man with a blind mind claims to be enlightened.

19

The Guru then turned toward Harydal, "I will not wear this thread. It is no more sacred than the cotton from which it is made."

All the guests were shocked. They all tried to persuade him to change his mind but he refused to yield.

The priest in utter despair, then asked, "What kind of sacred thread would you wear?"

> Out of the cotton of compassion
> Spin the thread of contentment,
> Tie knots of continence, give it the twist of truth.
> Make such a sacred thread for the mind,
> Such a thread once worn will never break
> Nor get soiled, burnt or lost.
> The Man who wears such a thread
> Is blessed.
> You buy a thread for pennies
> And seated in a plastered square
> Put it round the neck of others.
> Claiming an inheritance of holiness
> Your thread helps neither here nor hereafter.
> The wearer dies and leaves it behind.

The audience was hushed into silence by the truth of what Nanak had said. They felt that the regalia of sanctity without inner conviction was like dressing a thief in the clothes of holiness. They were overpowered by the wisdom and presence of the young Guru.

His father, however, under the spell of conventional religion, was deeply disappointed at his son's behavior in refusing to put on the sacred thread.

A PROFITABLE BARGAIN

The audacity of his young son's behavior had put the father to great ridicule and shame. In spite of the growing evidence of Nanak's spiritual greatness, he saw him only as a wayward boy, self-willed and headstrong, who was wasting his time in profitless contemplation.

He would be patient for awhile and then again devise a new way of interesting his son in learning the ways of the world.

One day he approached Nanak, lovingly patted him on the back, and said, "You should learn to make honest and profitable bargains. Take this money and go to the nearest market-place with your friend Bala and buy something in the cheapest market and sell it at the highest price. This is the way to make a real profit.

The Guru obeyed, and with his friend Bala, started out for the neighboring town. He left the main road, taking a short-cut through the uninhabited countryside. He had not gone very far when he saw a group of holy men seated under a grove of trees. He went straight to them and, bowing before the leader, sat near him and asked, "Why have you stopped in such a deserted place?"

"It may appear deserted to you,"'replied the leader, "but it is free from the shadow of the evil places from where you come."

"Our needs are few," he continued. "We do not require what the people in towns and villages require. God in His mercy provides for us as He provides for all."

"Pardon me for asking, but when did you have your last meal?" asked the Guru.

The leader smiled. "Some five days ago," he said. "Look at my companions. Do they show any signs of over-feeding? It's good to acquire control over the appetites of the body."

"Does control over the appetites of the body give one control over the mind?" asked the Guru.

"No, but it is the first step in controlling the mind," replied the leader.

This pleased the Guru and he thought nothing could be more profitable than to feed these good men who were hungry. He took out the money and, in spite of Bala's protests, placed it before the leader.

"My boy, take away this money which your father has given you for some other purpose. I have vowed never to touch money, only food."

"That's a good principle," said the Guru. "I'll go and bring you some food."

The Guru immediately got up and, with Bala, went to the nearest market to purchase provisions, which Bala still thought were being bought for a profitable transaction. On their way home, they again came across the holy men. The Guru stopped and laid before the leader all his purchases and without waiting for a reply started homeward followed by Bala.

Nanak stopped near a clump of trees near the otuskirts of the village and told Bala to go home. Obeying, he met Mehta Kalu, just as he entered the village, who asked him where his son was. Bala told him that he had left him near the village grove.

"Take me there," demanded Mehta Kalu.

Bala led him to the spot where he had left the Guru. They found him seated calmly, lost in meditation.

The father shook him angrily, and said, "What are you doing here? What have you done with the money?"

The Guru opened his eyes and looked him straight in the face but made no answer.

Mehta Kalu grew angrier and was about to slap him when Rai Bular appeared on the scene.

Kalu greeted him and said, "I am very upset. I gave my son some money this morning to go to town and make a profit and he has wasted it all and returned empty-handed."

"How has the money been wasted?" inquired Rai Bular, turning to Bala who was trembling with fear.

"Forgive me, sir," said Bala. "Nanak bought some food with the money and finding a group of holy men who had gone without food for many days, in spite of my protests, gave it to them."

"Why did you do it?" asked Kalu.

"Father, you asked me to strike a profitable bargain. What could have been of more profit to me, or to you, both in this world and the next, than feeding the hungry and the holy?"

Rai Bular, a man of real understanding, turned to Mehta Kalu and said, "Your son is not meant for gaining in this world. His gains are the gains of Heaven. Don't be angry with him, but let him follow his own way, for his way is the right way."

Kalu could say nothing. He bowed his head to Rai Bular, though he remained entirely unconvinced.

HIS WORRIED MOTHER

As Guru Nanak grew older, he would more and more avoid company and seek seclusion. He would remain for long hours in his room without eating or talking. At sixteen he had nothing in common with other boys his age. His mother was, of course, greatly concerned. She caressed him tenderly and tearfully begged him to follow his father's advice. "You are so wrapped up in yourself that people think you have lost your reason. They talk ill of you as of us. My darling, I want people to talk well of all of us. And, my son," she continued, "you must eat something, how can you live without food? What is this true Name of which you are constantly speaking?"

Nanak bowed with glistening eyes to his mother and said,

> To remember Him is to live
> To forget Him is to die.
> It is difficult to explain
> the true Name.
> When hunger for it
> Awakens in the heart
> All other hungers depart
> And this hunger consumes all suffering.
> O my mother!

The true Lord
How can He be named
He Whose Name is Truth?
The greatness of His true Name
Men's minds grow weary trying to grasp.
Their collective efforts are in vain.
His greatness cannot be over-stated.
Nor His greatness over-estimated.
He does not die nor is He mourned.
He is the giver,
The flow of His gifts is unending.

"How can one know Him?" asked his mother.

There is only this to know
There is no one but He
Neither in the past
Nor in the future.
He Who created the day
And then created the night,
His bounties are as boundless as He Himself.

"But they say that only people of great learning can approach Him," said his mother.
The Guru smiled and said,

They alone are of low birth
Who forget the true Master.
Without the grace of His Name
Their status is low.
There is no other distinction.

The mother and son continued to talk for a long time. The link of love drew him to his mother. He ate of the food which she placed before him and then, as if a new chord had been touched, he sang songs in praise of God.

WHO IS SICK?

Everyone was by now convinced that Nanak was beyond saving. Friends of the family shook their heads, saying that the poor boy was not normal. Others said he was possessed by spirits. His parents tried their best, but the Guru refused to give any explanations or alter his ways. The family thought that he might be sick and decided to get a doctor to examine him. Kalu summoned Hari Dass, the village physician, who sat down by Nanak and began to feel his pulse, but the "patient" withdrew his arm and, with a smile, said:

"They have sent for you, Doctor, to discover my disease. You need not put your hand on my pulse for the pain lies deep within my soul, not in my body. The disease I'm blessed with is that I'm in love, and He alone whose lover I am knows how to get me over it. Don't take care of me but of yourself. You cannot act as a physician unless you can first remove your own disease—the pain that disturbs your peace. Then you may treat others and call yourself a physician."

Hari Dass smiled cynically. He was familiar with cases of deranged minds. "So you think I am sick and need a cure?"

"Undoubtedly," said the Guru, "you suffer from sickness of the soul."

"And what would that sickness be?" asked Hari Dass.

The Guru looked at him with eyes full of compassion and said, "I-AM-NESS is the disease. It separates us not only from our fellow men, but from the source of life, God Himself."

"What are its symptoms?" Hari Dass asked.

The Guru answered,

> Separation is a constant source of pain,
> Hunger for union, another,
> The fear of the body perishing with disease,
> And the haunting fear of the Angel of Death.

Hari Dass was lost in wonder, for he knew inside that what the Guru said was true. He felt a strange peace stealing over him filling his heart and soul.

"You speak of things of the spirit. My concern is with the body alone."

The Guru turned his loving eyes on him and said, "Is the body worth anything without the spirit? Just as Sandalwood is valued only while it exhales perfume, the body is valued while it pulsates with life. It is cast away when breath leaves it; then your medicines are of no use."

"That's true," said the physician, "but how is it that this truth eludes mankind?"

"Listen," said the Guru.

> Man's mind, blind with desire,
> Sows the seed of its own suffering.
> Always indulging the self,
> It forgets God and undergoes endless suffering.
> Doctor, your medicine is of no help.

24

Suffering itself is the symptom of disease,
As well as its cure.

"Is there no help? Is there a cure?" asked Hari Dass.

Yes, disease and its cause can be cured.
By the saving grace of the true Name.
The bright and radiant Name
Of the Infinite, when it fills the mind
Banishes its impurities,
And transmutes it into pure gold.

Hari Dass forgot his role as a doctor. He sat spell-bound trying
to draw into his soul the aura of spirit which surrounded the Guru.
When he left, it was as a disciple. He told Mehta Kalu that his anxiety
about his son was useless, as he was a teacher and destined to follow
the way of all prophets.

HIS DEVOTED SISTER

Bibi Nanki, the Guru's married sister, came to visit her parents
with her husband, Jai Ram, who was an official in the service of the
Nawab, the Muslim deputy-governor, Daulat Khan. Devoted to her
younger brother, she was concerned about his drift toward unworld-
liness and her father's increasing impatience at the boy's indifference
toward all that he valued in the world—position and wealth.

She talked it over with her husband and mother and decided it
might help to bring her brother to her home in Sultanpur and to get
him a job in the Nawab's service. She approached her father with the
proposal. He said, "I am afraid you will spoil him with your love and
only encourage him to remain idle."

"No, father," she said, "I think that regular work will impress
upon him the daily needs of life. Then I'll arrange his marriage and,
having a wife to support, he will no longer be so indifferent to
money."

This, the father agreed, would tie him down to earth so much
that there would be no escape for him but to settle down as a man of
the world, if not for himself, at least for the sake of his wife and
children. And besides, the change of environment might do him good.
So he consented.

The day for Nanki to return home arrived and Nanak agreed to
go with her. Rai Bular gave a banquet in his honor and the whole
village came to see him off. Then, bowing at the feet of his father
and mother, he departed. The parents were happy that Nanak had
agreed at last to adopt the routine of the world.

When Nanak reached Sultanpur he was seventeen years old. His brother-in-law was able to get him a position in charge of a department which issued grain to the Nawab's servants. He raised no objections but took up his duty with a diligence which came as a happy surprise to his sister. After a time, this encouraged her to arrange his marriage. The Guru again raised no objections. He was married in due course and lived in a separate house with his wife and his two old friends, Bala, a Hindu, and Mardana, a Muslim. Both lived to serve the Guru and remained with him to the end.

For three years, the Guru lived the life of a householder and his wife gave birth to two sons. It seemed as if the purpose of the Guru was to demonstrate that the household was a school in which self-love was changed into love for others and earning an honest living was a pre-requisite to godliness.

In his capacity as store-keeper, he gave to all who asked for grain, according to their need, and yet the granaries were full. In the course of three years a rumor came to the attention of the Nawab that Nanak was squandering the royal stores, recklessly giving away grain and that the Nawab would find his granaries empty. It was said that when Nanak reached the figure "thirteen," while weighing out grain, he would endlessly repeat the Punjabi word for thirteen, "taira" which also meant "Yours," saying "Yours, O God, I am Yours."

The Nawab ordered an inquiry which was conducted with great care. Accounts were scrutinized. Grain was reweighed. Nanak's detractors were surprised when the stores were found full and accounts showed a balance in favor of the Guru.

The Guru, however, sent in his resignation. "Why have you resigned?" asked Jai Ram.

"My account is closed," said the Guru, "and with it my first mission has come to a close."

"What is your mission?" saked Jai Ram.

"To bring men nearer to God in order to enjoy the treasures of happiness," said the Guru.

"Where are the treasures of happiness in this world of suffering ing?" asked Jai Ram.

"They are within you," said the Guru. "But alas! it is the pomp and glory of the world, the puppet play of passion, which cheats man of his heritage and rewards him with suffering."

"Is renunciation of the world the way?" asked Jai Ram. "Are you going to become a monk?"

"No, my brother. Haven't I married and had sons? Haven't I lived the life of a householder? No, I am not going to become a monk, but show the way every householder can follow to attain liberation," said the Guru.

"Can you show me the way?" asked Jai Ram.

The Guru replied, "Haven't I shown it every day that I have lived with you? Now I will proclaim it to the world. I must go."

"So your mind is made up, " said Jai Ram. "What am I to tell your father and mother?"

"Tell them I am doing the work of the Father of all creation and my work will bring peace and comfort to them as to others."

He turned to go. His wife clung to him. "In whose care are you leaving me?" she sobbed through her tears.

"In the care of Him Who cares for all," he said and with these words, he put his hand on her head and her despair changed into calm content.

"Go," she said, bowing. "The world is in flames. Go and quench its fire."

JAP-JI

The Guru went out and sat on the bank of the river in a state of Samadhi—perfectly in tune with the cosmos. As he closed his eyes, the spirits of Kali Yug, the Age of Darkness, trembled at his appearance and let all their fury rage round him. Thunder, lightning and myriads of formless frightening shapes robed in blackness crowded round sharpening their five-pointed weapons of passion, anger, greed, delusion and conceit; emitting flames of desire and wielding the doubled-edged sword of hate and harm. He let them pass and remained calm like a lotus amidst stormy waters.

Then there passed before his mind palaces and pleasure domes flowing with milk and honey and swarming with maidens of unsurpassed beauty. The Guru smiled and sang:

> Pearl-built peerless palaces
> Adorned with precious gems
> Fragrant with all the scents of earth—
> These delude fools who forget His Name,
> Who have not Him in their hearts.
> My Master has told me
> There is no other place like His.

Then there passed before his eyes the richness of earth and all the treasured wealth that lies hidden under the sea and mountains. The Guru again smiled and sang:

27

Were earth blazing with diamonds,
And sparkling with rubies,
Overflowing with maidens of glamorous beauty,
These delude only fools
Who have not Him in their hearts.

Then, it seemed to him that the kingdom of earth was at his feet. He again smiled and sang:

What does it matter if I become a king,
And command mighty armies,
And occupy a golden throne,
And like the wind my commands encompass the earth?
These delude fools only
Who have not Him in their hearts.

Then it seemed as if he was tempted by the offer of supernatural powers and sovereignty over nature, but he rejected these with the remark,

If I exercise supernatural powers
And can create wealth at a gesture
Can appear and disappear at will
And thus win popular respect,
These delude fools only
Who have not Him in their hearts.

The Guru discarded all that the earth and heavens could offer and with his mind as calm as a placid lake, he lost himself in contemplation and became one with the Supreme.

Next morning people said they saw him walk straight into the river and disappear entirely from sight. It was thought that he had drowned and his sister and brother-in-law mournfully searched the water for his body.

The Guru, however, had ascended to the plane of Truth and appeared before the True One. On the third day he reappeared with a luminous aura around him. Crowds gathered and in a trance he pronounced the first principle of his faith—

Ek Ong Kar
Sat Nam
Karta Purkha
Nirbhau Nirvair
Akal Moorat Ajooni Sehbhang
Gur Prasad

Jap—

Aad Sach
Jugaad Sach
Hae Bhi Sach
Nanak Hosi Bhi Sach

There is but one God
Truth is His Name
Maker of all things
Free of fear and hate
Timeless, birthless, self-existent
Known by the grace of the Guru

Meditate on the True Name—

True in the beginning
True in all ages
He is true now
And he shall ever be true, says Nanak.

He is True and His Name is true
He is and He shall be
He who has arranged
This play of the Universe,
This material world,
In various forms and hues.
He shall never pass away.
He enjoys the sight of His own artistry,
To His own Eternal Glory.
He is the all-powerful,
Subject to no other command.
He is the Lord of lords, the King of kings,
All live under His will.

In a state of ecstasy, he continued.

You are all wisdom, omniscient,
Deeper than the oceans,
How could a fish ascertain
The limits of an ocean.
You are everywhere,
Wherever I look,
There you are.
Separated from you,
Like a fish I die.
I know not the fisherman
I know not the noose of his net.
I am aware of only one thing,
He is everywhere,
He is not far away,
All acts are performed
In his presence.
He sees all.
Men forget to serve Him
Or to remember His Name.
They enjoy what He gives.
There is no door but His door.
Nanak the suppliant says
My soul and body are His sacrifice.

Then raising his eyes, he pronounced an Invocation.

You are near, you are far,
You are all in all,
You see, you hear

You create this Universe,
What pleases You,
That is the only right action.

Thus imbued with the spirit of God, the Guru turned toward the
the town to again kindle the hearts of others with the love of the
Lord which burned in his own.

 ### THERE IS NO HINDU OR MUSLIM

The Guru walked to the village cemetery and sat down in a soli-
tary spot. Men and women came to see him, making all kinds of re-
marks. Some said a ghost had taken hold of him and others that he
had lost his mind. The Guru answered,

Foolish people think ghosts have possessed me
Others with pity pronounce my name.
They know little of God-intoxication.
Nanak is possessed with the love of God and nothing else.

Jai Ram was deeply distressed. He consulted a Maulvi, a Muslim
priest, who was held in great esteem. The Maulvi said he would cure
Nanak and exorcise the evil spirit. He came and sat down in front of
the Guru and began his incantations. The Guru turned to him and
said,

They whose crop is ruined in the field
What can they gather on the threshing floor?
Accursed are they who write and sell God's Name.

The Maulvi, however, continued asking the spirit that possessed
Nanak to declare itself. The Guru laughed and said,

This foolish world thinks
He in whose heart
Dwells fear of God,
Who acknowledges
No other but Him,
Who submits to His will,
Is mad.
Is this the mark of wisdom?

"You talk like a wise man," said the Maulvi, "but you act like a
fool."

"How do you reconcile the two?" asked Nanak. "You consider me mad because I regard as valueless what men like you value."

> He
> Whose heart is filled
> With the love of the Lord,
> Who considers himself
> Less than the dust
> And all others his betters—
> Can such a one lack sanity?

"So you are sane and I believe it," said the Maulvi. "Your abnormal behavior is not due to any external cause but your own will. What is your purpose in abandoning your home?"

The Guru got up and declared, "To serve mankind. There is no Hindu. There is no Muslim."

The priest turned to Jai Ram and said, "There is nothing wrong with Nanak."

Jai Ram paid him and he departed. In the meantime Nanki and the Guru's wife arrived. "Dear brother," said Nanki, "why have you abandoned your home, wife and sons and taken your residence in this dreadful place?"

"Isn't this the place where eventually everybody must come?" the Guru replied. "I have come to it of my own will instead of on the shoulders of other men. They who ignore the truth that this mortal body must perish are indeed foolish.

Nanki again appealed to her brother to think of his family and not leave them.

The Master replied, "My dear sister, humanity is my family and in serving it I serve you also."

The news that the Guru had reappeared and had said, "There is no Hindu and no Muslim," reached the Nawab.

The Nawab's Qazi, or minister, demanded that the Guru should be summoned and required to explain his sweeping assertion which, the Qazi said, bordered on heresy.

"He could say what he wished about his own religion, but he had no right to talk lightly of Islam," he added.

A messenger was dispatched to bring the Guru to the Court of the Nawab. As he approached Nanak, he was so overwhelmed by the spirit of peace pervading the Guru that he humbly said, "Sir, the Nawab shall be very pleased if you grace his Court with your presence."

The Guru answered, "My brother, I have no concern with the Nawab now. I am in the service of Him, who is the Sovereign of this World."

32

The messenger returned and reported the conversation. The Qazi rose angrily and said, "I will bring this heretic myself to your presence."

The Qazi, as he approached the Guru, seemed to lose mastery over himself and in spite of his resolution respectfully said, "Nanak, come with me. The Nawab is anxious to be enlightened by you."

"If he seeks light, I cannot refuse the summons," said the Guru and accompanied him.

The Nawab was a great believer in saints. Nanak's administration of his store-house, his disappearance and reappearance had greatly impressed him. He rose to receive the Guru and gave him a seat next to himself.

"I am puzzled," he said, "by your statement that there is no Hindu and no Muslim. Isn't my Qazi a true Muslim? Am I not a humble follower of the Prophet?"

"My dear Nawab, it is very difficult indeed to be a Muslim," said the Guru.

The Qazi turned on him with flashing eyes and said, "What do you mean?"

The Guru answered, as was his practice, in a song:

> He who is firm in his faith
> Has a right to be called a Muslim.
> His acts must accord with his faith in the Prophet.
> He must clean his heart of pride and greed,
> No more troubled by the two impostors—life and death.
> Resigned to the will of God,
> Knowing Him as the Doer,
> Freed from the domination of the self,
> Compassionate to all things
> Such a one may call himself a Muslim.

The Qazi was not prepared to accept this definition and asked, "What are you?"

"I am neither a Muslim nor a Hindu," answered the Guru.

"Why?" asked the Qazi.

The Guru said, "Only he has a right to call himself religious, who lives in the light of God's word brought to earth by prophets of all religions. To me all religions are His."

The time for prayer had come, so the Nawab intervened, "If all religions are the same to you, will you join us in offering prayers?"

"With pleasure," answered the Guru, "if you or the Qazi will lead the prayer."

The Nawab and the Qazi rose and the Guru accompanied them.

The news rapidly spread that Nanak had entered the mosque to offer prayers with the Nawab. Nanak's family and other Hindus were greatly upset. They thought he was about to be converted so they all rushed to the mosque where he was to offer prayers and waited at its gates.

It was Friday and a large congregation of Muslims had assembled. The Qazi stood first, behind him the Nawab and then Nanak and other prominent persons, and behind them the rest of the people. When prayers were offered and the faithful kneeled, Nanak remained standing and took no part in the service.

When it was over, the Qazi in an angry mood turned to Nanak, "You are an impostor," he said. "You said you would pray with us and you remained standing."

I promised to offer prayers under your leadership," said Nanak. "Since you were not praying, how could I?"

The Qazi turned to the Nawab and said, "Have you ever heard such blasphemy?"

The Nawab turned to the Guru and asked, "What is your explanation?"

"Now tell me, does praying merely consist in kneeling and bowing?" inquired the Guru.

"No," said the Qazi. "It is merely the outer expression of humility."

"Then tell me what is the inner expression?" the Guru said.

"The worship that the spirit offers," the Qazi replied.

"That is why I said neither you nor the Nawab were praying, for while your body was bowing your spirit was occupied with other things—both yours and that of the Nawab," said the Guru.

"What things?" countered the Qazi angrily.

"You were thinking of your mare which had just foaled and you were afraid that the foal might fall into the well which is in your courtyard. Am I right?"

The Qazi held down his head for it was true.

"And me?" asked the Nawab humbly.

"Your thoughts were not rising up to God either," said the Guru. "You were absorbed in the horses which your agents are purchasing in Kabul."

The Nawab bowed and said the Guru was right and the whole congregation was struck dumb with amazement.

The Guru then turned to the congregation. "I will tell you how to offer prayers and follow the holy script of the Koran."

> In the Mosque of love
> Spread the carpet of faith,
> Enjoy only your rightful earnings,
> Follow the holy script.
> Make restraint and modesty your circumcision,

Moderation your fast,
Right action your pilgrimage to Mecca.
Make truth your spiritual guide,
Good works your creed,
Thus become a Muslim.
Repeat His Name on your rosary,
He will exalt you."

"Listen, people! I speak the truth. Learn to realize the meaning of prayers, purify your minds so that the words may acquire power and become significant," said Nanak.

After taking his leave of the Nawab, Nanak returned home to say good-bye to his family.

"Where are you going?" they asked.

"I am going to serve my Master," he said, standing in the court-yard. "Wherever He bids me there I go."

The Guru cast eyes filled with love on the members of his family and their distress was changed into joy. Then, when they were at peace, he quietly walked away.

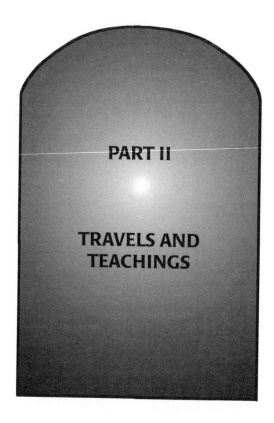

PART II

TRAVELS AND
TEACHINGS

Accompanied by Bala and Mardana, the Guru left Sultan-pur. They had not gone far when he turned to Mardana and said, "Go to the North where you will meet a friend who will give you a Rubab."

"But, Sir," said Mardana, "I have no friend there and have never played on the Rubab."

The Guru looked at him with the light of love in his eyes and said, "Do as I tell you and discover for yourself the truth of what I am saying."

The kindly eye that met Mardana convinced him that the Guru was sincere. He immediately obeyed and headed in the direction the Guru had indicated. He had just crossed a hedge when an old man with a white beard and a bright beautiful face greeted him and asked him what he was looking for.

"A Rubab," said Mardana.

"So Nanak has sent you," said the old man. "Tell him that Farenda, his servant, has carried out his command. Blessed are they who have the privilege of his divine company. Here is the Rubab I have carried for you for many years."

Mardana grasped the beautiful guitar-like instrument and turned in gratitude to Farenda only to find that he had disappeared.

He took the Rubab and returned to the Guru marveling at the miracle.

"Now take the Rubab and play," said the Guru.

"I have never played, Sir," he pleaded.

"You were a master player," said the Guru, "and once you run your fingers over it, your skill will come back to you in a flash."

Mardana obeyed. His fingers began to move automatically and poured forth divine music. The Guru accompanied him with a hymn:

If I live millions of years
On air alone,
Sun and moon
No more mark the time,
I could not even then describe Your greatness.
You, the changeless,
The formless,
Men speak of You
Within the limits of their power.
If there were millions
Of pounds of paper
And ink without end,
And a pen driven by the wind,
Even then Your greatness
Could not be expressed.
How can I exact Your Name?

FOOD FOR THOUGHT

It was nearly sunset when Guru Nanak started on his journey with the Muslim minstrel and the Hindu attendant which symbolized his universal spirit.

The Guru stopped at Sayadpur and stayed at the house of a poor carpenter named Lalo, who welcomed him with great humility and reverence.

It happened at that time that Malik Bhago, the "Dewan" or local governor, was giving a sacrificial feast and expected all religious and holy men to come.

The news that a saint was staying at the house of Lalo reached Malik Bhago. He immediately sent a servant to invite the Guru and his followers. The Guru, however, refused to accept the invitation. Bhago, believing that his feast would be incomplete unless all holy men graced his house, sent his servants to force Nanak to come if he refused again. At first the Guru refused to budge, but then thinking that this might be a good occasion to teach a lesson agreed to go. But when he reached his host's palace and was offered food, he declined to eat. When asked why he was insulting Bhago so in the presence of the whole assembly when he had felt no qualms about eating the food cooked by an untouchable carpenter, the Guru calmly replied: "Give me some food cooked in this house, and I will show you."

The Guru asked Lalo also to get some food from his house. In the meantime a great crowd had gathered around the Guru.

When food from the two houses was brought, the Guru took a piece which came from Lalo's house in his right hand and some food from Bhago's house in his left and squeezed the two. From Lalo's food drops of milk oozed out and from Bhago's drops of blood.

"Now you see why I refused to eat your food," said the Guru. "Your food is blood-stained and drawn from others. Lalo enjoys what he earns by the sweat of his brow and out of it shares what little he can with others. No sanctified ritual can make your food pure."

Bhago fell at the Guru's feet and prayed for mercy.

"Listen," said the Guru.

> That which belongs to another
> Is unlawful like the flesh of a pig
> To a Muslim and cow's flesh to a Hindu.
> The Guru and Pir will extend their grace
> If you refrain from eating meat.
> Meat does not become lawful
> By breathing God's Name over it.
> Nor do we secure paradise
> By indulgence in holy talk.
> The fruit of false talk is falsehood.
> Only good deeds open the road to salvation.

The news traveled throughout the countryside that a teacher had appeared who challenged caste and authority with a fearlessness never known before.

 "LIVING IN THE WORLD"

On the outskirts of Sialkat, away from all human habitation, the Guru rested.

Puzzled, Mardana asked, "Why do you prefer the wilderness to the comforts of the town?"

"There is no comfort in a place where there is no truth," replied the Guru. "The air of the town is charged with hypocrisy. Who could safely breathe it?"

Mardana pleaded that he was hungry and could not live on the wild air that blew about him.

"Take this slip of paper," said the Guru. "Enter the city and show it to rich and poor alike. He who answers the questions which I have written on it will give you food." They were—'What is real? What is unreal.'

Mardana walked through the town showing his slip of paper to rich and poor alike. They refused to look at it and laughed at him, till he reached the shop of a baker who took the paper and wrote a reply, "Death is real and living is unreal." Then he served Mardana food. When Mardana had satisfied his hunger, the baker asked to be taken to the person who had written the questions. The baker, when he saw the Guru, humbly bowed before him and asked, "Show me the true way, O searcher of hearts!"

"Seek and you will find it. It is found by search and lost by discussion," said the Guru.

The baker was so impressed by the Guru that he accompanied him for many days, till the Guru ordered him to go back.

"I want to be a wandering ascetic—a Fakir," pleaded the baker. "I wish to give up the world."

"Listen," said the Guru. "It is not by shirking our duty that we become saints, but by daily performance of that which is ordained. We learn the beginning of self-denial by denying ourselves for the sake of our family, by active sympathy with suffering, and forbearance for all."

"Then why is it that people leave their homes in search of God?" asked the baker.

"There are true seekers and selfish escapists," said the Guru, "but my way lies in living in the world and rising step by step steadily and surely, by purification of the mind by daily conflict with the force that darkens the light of the soul. This is only possible if we do our day-to-day duties with the Name of God on our lips, so that all our actions are performed in the service of Him who is the Lord of all that exists."

The Guru then repeated the opening passage of Jap-ji and said, "Meditate on this, try to reach the inner meaning, then the true desire in your heart will gain strength and you will become a devotee. The light of the Beloved will illumine your innermost being. Remember, renunciation of outward things does not make for inner righteousness. Words are meaningless till translated into action."

The baker repeated the opening passage of the Jap-ji after the Guru and understood its meaning. He then returned to his shop, lived the life of a householder with the Name of God on his lips, animated by a spirit of service which made life a blessing for all. A friend of Hindus and Muslims alike, he saw God in the temple and in the mosque and found service of his fellow man the truest method of worship.

Guru Nanak wandered from village to village opening up hearts to Truth regardless of caste or religion. He came to a place where a notorious thief called Sajjan, meaning "a good friend," lived. Sajjan always dressed in pure white, wore the sacred Hindu mark on his forehead and a Muslim rosary around his neck. He had built a Hindu temple and a Muslim mosque at his gate and invited travelers to his residence where he then robbed them. Sajjan was always on the watch for victims and so when he saw Nanak and his companions, he rejoiced, for they looked both innocent and defenseless. The thief invited them to his home and the Guru accepted with a twinkle of amusement in his eye.

When night fell the Guru asked Mardana to play the Rubab and invited Sajjan to come and listen to his songs. Sajjan agreed. Mardana's fingers wandered over the strings and the music touched the thief's heart. Then the Guru began his song.

> Bronze is bright and shining,
> Rub it and it turns black
> And a hundred washings cannot remove it.
> They are sajjans, they are true comrades
> Whose friendship bears the mark of sincerity,
> Who are present in a friend's hour of need.
> A sacred peepal tree in the courtyard,
> A Dharamsala at the gate,
> Attractive in outer appearance but hollow within,
> The red marks of sanctity on the forehead
> And a rosary round the neck,
> Deceitful disguises to cheat the world.
> Houses and mansions decorated and painted,
> They will be of little use; they must crumble away.
> Men clad in white like herons wait for their victims
> At places of pilgrimage and follow a wicked trade.
> They are not sajjans, they are not good friends
> But like the seemal tree that attracts birds
> By its brilliant flowers but is without fruit,
> It sends them back hungry and unsatisfied.
> So men without virtue are like trees without fruit.
> They blindly load themselves with sin
> Knowing not that the road is long and dreary
> And those heavy-laden with sin
> Have to cross the dreary road,
> Blinded and without sight; they cannot ascend the heights.
> Labor, cunning and craft are of no avail.

Nanak says
Remember God and find release from the prison of self.

Sajjan Realized the Guru's words were addressed to him and were entering his heart like shafts of light and demanding repentance. He was overwhelmed with the consciousness of his misdeeds. A picture of all that he had done passed before his mind's eye. He fell at the Guru's feet and begged to be saved.

Tears flowed from his eyes. The Guru raised Sajjan's head and said, "There is no cause for despair for God is merciful and reads the heart. You must truly repent and reform your life"

"Tell me and I will do what you bid me," said Sajjan. "You must recall all the wrongs you have done one by one and then repent from the depth of your heart. Repentance is not a mere repeating of a formula, it is recognition of wrong and driving out tendencies that lead to wrong-doing. The next thing you must do is to find the persons you have wronged and to repay them and seek their forgiveness. The days you spend in redressing wrongs will be the days of your redemption." Then the Guru taught him the first stanza of the Jap-ji and how to feel the presence of God whether awake or asleep.

Sajjan obeyed and spent long days finding his victims and repaying them. He suffered indignities and abuse, but remained firm with God's Name on his lips and became a true devotee of the Guru.

"NOTHING THAT LIVES EVER DIES"

The Guru continued year after year to spread light to the farthest village. One day he suddenly exclaimed: "My friend, Rai Bular, wants me; his journey on this earth is coming to an end. I must see him." He immediately retraced his steps homeward and went straight to Rai Bular's house. Bala and Mardana meanwhile visited their own families, and informed the Guru's parents of their son's return. When Rai Bular saw the Guru, he tried to rise from his bed but could not do so. "My spirit is at your feet but the flesh is weak," he murmured slowly.

The old man's devotion touched the heart of the Guru who rushed to him and put his hand on his shoulder and said, "The message of your spirit has reached my heart. It has brought me to you."

With tears in his eyes, Rai Bular prayed that as he could not rise and touch his feet, the Guru should touch his head with his feet so that he might obtain salvation.

The Guru put his hand on the dying man's head and he felt as if his soul was finally released from the cycle of birth and death. A strange peace entered his heart and with its co ning the breath of life departed.

The Guru's father and mother, when they heard of his arrival, rushed to see him. His mother with tears of joy took some sweets for him. Seeing Nanak dressed like a Fakir, his father said, "Son, take my horse and go back home. I'm upset at the way you look, the son of a proud householder wandering like a beggar." Nanak humbly replied, "Father, the horses are of no use to me. He who knows his way does not go another. He whose glory shines in the Presence of God by His Grace feels himself to be the king of the world."

Distressed at hearing these words, Kalu said, "If I only knew what had disappointed you in life, I would set things right. If you want to marry another woman, I'd get you one, if another house, I'd provide you with it." Nanak replied, "God alone have I married. It is He who controls me controls everyone in the world—each to his own task. And whosoever else errs, God does not." Nanak then said that he must leave and without stopping even a day, resumed his wanderings, consoling his parents that he would see them again when they wanted him.

"You are very strange," said Mardana when they stopped for a rest. "You came all this way to see Rai Bular whom you called your friend and yet when he died, you did not even shed a tear."

"Listen," said the Guru to Mardana, "those in whose heart God dwells return to their heavenly home. Death is nothing but a gateway to birth. Nothing that lives ever dies, it only changes form. You see the tree under which you sit, how its leaves have withered. After a short time it will be covered with fresh ones. Similarly, when a man's body is weary the soul leaves the body to receive newer and fresher garments. And so on goes this great play of God—from eternity to eternity."

 ## THE VILLAGE OF GOD

Throughout his journey the Guru spoke to Hindus and Muslims alike. They gathered around him like bees round a honeycomb. He made no attempt to proselytize but people received his gospel in all sincerity and became his disciples. The Guru completed his tour of the villages and cities of the Punjab and then came and stayed at a place on the banks of the Ravi not far from Batala. People flocked to him: Hindus, Muslims, sadhus, fakirs, the depressed classes. In the morning they heard sweetly sung hymns and the Guru's teachings.

The good news spread far and wide that where the Guru dwelt, falsehood found no place, truth was proclaimed and only the Sacred Name of God was expounded.

A rich banker who was the owner of the area and a Muslim resented an infidel becoming so popular. He decided to go and tell the

Guru to leave his land. He mounted his horse and started off with his following. He had not gone far when his horse stumbled and he fell headlong on the ground. He suffered no serious injury but his followers brought him back home.

He rested for a couple of days and then again he started off to expel the Guru. He had not gone beyond the gate of his house when he realized that his sight was gone. He dismounted and returned home amazed at this strange occurrence.

"How has this happened?" he asked his followers.

"Nanak is a holy man," they said, "and you were going with the intention of expelling him, so God did not allow you to proceed."

"I will show him all respect," he said, and mounted his horse again but as he proceeded he lost his sight again.

"What am I to do?" he asked his followers.

"Sir you must go on foot," said his followers. "Purge your heart of anger and humbly beg his forgiveness before starting."

The banker humbly prayed that he might be forgiven and started on foot. His sight was restored and he reached the place where the Guru had settled.

He saw the Guru seated calmly, surrounded by people. The sweet music that was being played filled him with an indescribable peace.

He fell at the feet of the Guru, who affectionately asked him to take a seat near him. This mere act completely changed the banker and awakened in him the desire to serve the Guru. He got up and said, "My true teacher! I am blessed at the sight of you. I know I am forgiven. Permit me to dedicate all this area to you. You can found a village."

The Guru smiled, and said, "The land is of Kartar—God—and you are blessed for dedicating it to divine service. We shall call the village Kartarpur, the place of Kartar."

In a short while Kartarpur grew in importance. Dharamsalas—inns for pilgrims—and houses were built and the Guru's family moved to the village. It was from there that the Guru went out again on his long journeys.

Kartarpur became the headquarters of the Guru. Amidst chanting of the hymns, morning and evening, and discourses by the Guru, the congregation grew larger and larger and the free kitchen fed all who came.

The Guru started a small farm, which he worked himself. He held that the right way to live was by one's own labor. The Guru produced enough for himself and his family and gave the surplus to the free kitchen.

He set the example of leading a simple householder's life and realizing the spirit of true religion, devoted to God and the service of his fellow-men, combining simple life with lofty thoughts, free from shams, hypocrisies and metaphysical pursuits which keep the mind from truth. By his own example he showed that by righteous living, even amidst gaiety and laughter, salvation could be attained.

LAHORE – A VILE CITY

It was time for another journey. With his two old companions, Guru Nanak started for Lahore. He found the city's narrow and dirty streets and the large number of slaughtered animals, which provided meat for the inhabitants, deeply disturbing. The unrelieved poverty of the working classes and ostentatious luxury of the rich impressed him so much that he exclaimed, "The city of Lahore seethes with poisonous oppression."

He left the town for he could not endure its stifling atmosphere. But he could not forget what he had seen. Full of pity for the people he expressed his feelings in a song.

> Sin occupies the throne,
> With greed the financier,
> Falsehood the commander,
> Lust and desire as the judges
> Who summon and examine men
> And pronounce judgments.
> The people in their ignorance
> Are without power.
> They too are eager to usurp
> What others have.
> Priests have forgotten their craft.
> They dance, wear masks,
> Beat drums and adorn their bodies.
> They shout aloud, indulge in battle songs, and uphold war.
> Ignorant Pandits with subtle-reasoning
> And tricks of their trade strip men and amass wealth.
> Even those who perform good acts do so
> In a vain hope of obtaining salvation.
> The ascetics without true knowledge
> Leave their hearths and homes.
> Everyone considers himself perfect
> But if put to the test, says Nanak,
> Not one could prove true.

The Guru left Lahore and headed for Talwandi. On his way he stood outside a village temple watching worshippers offering flowers and tinkling temple bells.

One of the worshipers, seeing the Guru standing thoughtfully as an interested spectator, accosted him. "What are you looking at," he said, "go in and worship the God inside."

The Guru smiled and said, "Are you not aware of the God within you?"

> Repeat the Name of Rama
> And thus perform inner worship.
> Meditate upon the Word of the True Teacher,
> He is all-pervading.
> How can I worship in temples other gods
> When I see only the One and no other?"

"Do you come every day to worship?" inquired the Guru.

"No," said the man, "but this is the twelfth day of the lunar month and therefore after fasting yesterday I am worshiping God to acquire merit."

"My dear friend," said the Guru, "under what delusions are you laboring? You think because you visit the temple and offer a few flowers, you have done a religious duty. The twelfth day would be blessed if you were to give in charity, inspired by a true feeling of compassion, if you were to control the outgoing mind and restrain it within. Fasting from food is a mere penance. We fast truly when we renounce the fruit of our action. We pray truly when we repeat the Name of God and hear it repeated from within, and thus realize that the One pervades the three worlds. True worship is rendered by knowing the real from the unreal."

The worshiper fell at the feet of the Guru and asked for more advice.

"My friend, know this truth, that God is in every heart and every heart is His temple. It is through His blessings that we can approach Him, then the heart loses its hardness and it is filled with His love. By meditation the sense of duality is lost and individual being becomes one with the Supreme Being. By the favor of the Guru, this way is found. The heart is linked with God. Time no more rings down that curtain that we call death."

"ASSALAM ALAIKUM – PEACE BE WITH YOU"

At Pakpattan the travelers rested under a tree outside the town. Mardana tuned the Rubab and the Guru began to sing:

> You Yourself are the writing tablet,
> You the pen and You the writer.

You are also the written word,
You are the One. There is no other.

The shrine of Sheik Farid-ud-Din , a great Muslim Sufi of the
13th century was at Pakpattan. The custodian of the shrine was
Sheik Behram, called the second Farid, and the head of a school of
Sufis. A disciple of the Sheik , who came to collect fuel for his mas-
ter's kitchen, heard the hymn, and was deeply moved by its spirit.
He came and sat near the Guru.

He was so impressed that, on his return, he reported to his master that there was a saint sitting under a tree with his two disciples.
The strange part of it was that he looked like a Hindu while he who
played the Rubab looked like a Muslim and sang of the oneness of
God.

The Sheik was interested and told his disciple, "Go and ask
this question. There is one God but there are two ways. Which should
we accept and which reject?"

The disciple returned, bowed respectfully, and repeated the
question. The Guru smiled and said, "There is only one God and
there is only one way, stick to the one and reject the other."

Sheik Behram was greatly struck by the directness of the
answer and decided to go and see the Guru himself. He came and
greeted Nanak with "Assalam Alaikum"—peace be with you. The
Guru answered, "I salute the One and the Indescribable within you."

"Your reply is mysterious," said the Sheik . "The Hindus deny
the God of Islam and Muslims accuse the Hindus of worshiping many
gods. Yet you say, there is only one God and the one way."

"There is no mystery about it," answered the Guru. "The ignorant impose their own darkness on the light of Truth. They who see
divisions do not know God. Those who know Him proclaim His oneness."

God is one
He is not subject to change.
His light is the life of creation.
That which is born and dies
Cannot be the object of worship.
Worship the one God,
Who pervades water and earth.

The Sheik was very pleased. "I am indeed blessed at the sight
of you. I feel I could discard my robes and wrap myself in a rough
blanket or wear that which would bring me near to my Lord."

The Guru smiled sweetly and said:

47

Why discard clothes
And wrap yourself in a blanket
If your heart is pure and your devotion intense.
God Himself will grace your home

"My dear Sheik," he continued, "know the truth. These outer forms are of no account. It is the inner grace that counts. It is not necessary to dress as a beggar or to leave home. The one thing necessary is to remove the impurities of the mind, and fill the heart with longing to receive His grace. Just as the true desire of a woman, her faith and devotion, draws the beloved to her, so does a devotee draw the Lord by his true-hearted consecration to His service. The power of a growing love is great. Remember, the spark of true love is never lit in the heart till it is empty of self and filled with faith, fidelity and devotion. God Himself cannot resist the love of a devotee. He manifests Himself to his devotee who is then aware only of the Beloved."

The Sheik was deeply moved. "The man who fails to realize God is like the woman," he said, "whose desire is unquenched and who even in her grave cries for her heart's desire, for union."

"The Supreme Lord cares little for looks, dress or appearance," said the Guru. "A pure life, kindled with true devotion wins His approval. If I were asked, how I would dress myself to meet the Lord, my answer would be with sweetness of speech and cultivation of virtue. So richly attired I would allure the Lord. Humility in action, forgiveness in conduct and words that are like balm are true adornments of the soul. They win favor in the divine presence for all times. They who are of humble behavior, without any pride of self, forebearing and helpful, overlooking the faults of others, harmless in action and speech are on the path of achievement."

The Sheik exclaimed, "You are a true teacher, you are of God and God is in you. May I ask you another question?"

"What need is there for a question?" answered the Guru. "The devotees of God think and speak nothing else but of God. As beauty of form attracts the passionate, food the hungry, wealth the greedy, bed the weary and abuses the angry, so does a devotee dwell in silence on God. We must remember that this earth is not our permanent home. In eating, drinking, laughing and sleeping we forget death. Selfish desires and bodily comforts rob us of our power to seek the feet of the Lord. We must remember that life here is transitory. We must prepare for the other side."

"It is easy to speak of God," said the Sheik. "It is not so easy to kindle the heart with true devotion."

"Listen!" said the Guru. Sheik Farid has said:

They indeed are true-hearted
In whose heart dwells nothing but love of God.
They who have one thing in their hearts,
Another on their lips,
Are immature and unripe.
They forget Him
And only burden this weary earth.
They are truly imbued with the Divine
Who stand straight in His sight,
Like beggars at His gate,
With love of the Lord in their hearts.
Blessed is the mother
Who begot them,
Blessed the earth,
For they are its ripe fruit.
The Lord is timeless and unknowable,
He is all-forgiving.
Those who know this truth
Like Farid, receive the gift of love as alms.
I kiss their feet.
Take refuge in them.

"HE ALONE IS PERMANENT"

From Pakpattan the Guru moved on to Multan which was known as a great center of Sufis. The Guru sat near the mausoleum of Pir Baha-ud-Din, which was then in the charge of a celebrated Sufi who was acknowledged as Pir—a teacher and leader of a certain rank. The news that a wandering saint had stopped there reached him and he sent one of his disciples to the Guru with a cup filled to the brim with milk.

The messenger came and without a word presented the cup to the Guru. The Guru smiled, picked up a jasmine and placed it on the cup full of milk and told the messenger to take it back to his master.

Mystified, Mardana inquired, "What is the meaning of all this?"

"The Pir," said the Guru, "meant that Multan was as full of saints as the cup of milk and there was no room for another. I told him that I would be like the jasmine that floats on the overflowing cup."

The answer pleased the Pir, who came to meet the Guru with some of his disciples. The Guru got up to receive him and after greeting each other they sat down.

"From where have you come?" inquired the Pir, "and what is your religion?"

"I have come from where we all come. From Him who is the source of all existence. I belong to His religion."

"Do you believe that all is from Him?" asked the Pir with a twinkle in his eye.

The Guru looked straight into his eyes and said, "Only he, who has seen Him, can say with confidence that He is all and everything comes from Him."

"I would not have asked you," answered the Pir, "unless I was sure that you were in communion with Him. There is an aura around your head, which is light itself."

"Know this," said the Guru, "that for those who realize Him nothing exists but God. But as long as the sense of self remains, the world's sense of separateness from reality does not disappear. When the barriers of self are broken, He is seen within and without and reality is realized. He is not far. He is near. He pervades the whole creation. He is the One, there is nothing else, only the One who pervades everything."

"Tell me how this world came into being," asked the Pir.

"Need you know this?" answered the Guru. "Is it not more important to destroy the sense of separateness in which the world exists and attain union with God? It is only then you can find an answer to why and how."

The Pir was profoundly moved and rose to kiss Nanak's hands.

"Listen my friends," said the Guru, "it is through the sacred Word that we rise from consciousness of self to universal consciousness, and in that union we see only Him. Great are His powers, greater indeed are his gifts. All living beings, big and small, praise Him day and night. It is in the company of true seekers—the righteous, endowed with virtue—that the true path is discovered. Fear and hate which agitate the mind are destroyed and, out of limitless compassion, the true Lord raises the weak human being and makes him His own. The only way to find the path is to approach the perfect devotees who have become His. We need only know how and in what virtuous ways they realized Him. They will tell you that they adorned themselves with the virtue of self-surrender and its fruits—contentment, peace and sweet speech. For a true devotee, there exists nothing but God, but to become a devotee, perfect purification is required. It is only then that a devotee can dedicate himself to God."

The Pir sent his disciples away and then asked, "You have spoken of the Name, the sacred Word. What power is inherent in the Name of God?"

The Guru spoke, "The whole universe flowed from sound, the sound formed itself into the sacred Name. The sacred Name is the first manifestation of the unmanifest, in it all that is has its beginning. It is the one word that leads the manifest to the unmanifest."

The Pir asked, "Can you prove the power of the Word to reabsorb and recreate?"

The Guru smiled and said, "Calm yourself," and with these words he put his hand on the head of the Pir and uttered the divine Word, and in an instant the Pir was reduced to ashes. Again the Guru looked at the ashes and uttered the Word and the Pir appeared sitting in his place, saying, "La-Ilaha-Illa-Allah."

The Pir fell at the Guru's feet and begged him to teach him the way to salvation. The Guru gave him his blessings. After a few days Nanak decided to move on, but the Pir requested him to stay. He answered:

> It would be right to make a permanent home
> And escape the pain of daily wandering,
> If there were a permanent place
> And this world were unchanging.
>
> What kind of place is this world?
> Impermanent and transitory.
> It is wise to cling to the light of the Name
> And keep ready for the journey.
>
> Yogis perform postures.
> The Mullas dwell in holy places.
> The Pandits expound sacred books.
> The Sidhs occupy the abode of the gods.
>
> Demi-gods, Sidhs, Pirs and Sheiks,
> Heavenly Musicians and Munis,
> Saints, sages and commanders
> Have all to depart.
>
> Emperors, kings, princes and nobles
> Have all to march away.
> Man has no abiding place on earth.
> Understand, Man! You too must go.
>
> This truth has been repeatedly revealed
> Yet few pay heed to the truth.
> Nanak humbly asserts
> The permanent pervades on waters and earth.
>
> Allah, the unseen, the inscrutable,
> The omnipotent, the creator, the merciful,
> Is alone permanent.
> The whole world is in a state of flux.

He alone is permanent
Who is freed from the bondage of cause and effect.
The heavens and earth shall pass;
He, the Compassionate One, is permanent.

The sun travels by day,
The moon by night.
Hundreds and thousands of stars are moving.
He alone is permanent, says Nanak.

With these words the Guru bade an affectionate farewell to the Pir and resumed his journey.

THE GREAT ONES OF THE WORLD

Next, the Guru came to a place near Pasrur and decided to stop in a grove of fruit trees. A great Muslim Sufi by the name of Mian Mitha lived nearby and came out to see him, more with the idea of testing him than the desire for spiritual communion. A crowd gathered around them to hear the conversation between the two men of God.

"Tell me, you who seem so wise," asked Mian Mitha, "whom does God like?"

The Guru said, "In His court, high and low, rich and poor, all are alike. He who is true to the core and humble in his behavior gains the favor of the most high."

"What about the great ones of the world?" inquired the Sufi.

"They are like an elephant," the Guru said, "who feeds on butter and sweets, trumpets in its pride of strength and throws dust over its head, then lies in dust when death overtakes it. Good men are like birds, fluttering in the air, full of joy, content with the little that meets their needs and which God provides. An egoist enjoying sense objects may excite attention but the barb of the ego gives him no peace. His suffering is equal to his wrongful living. It is the humble and the meek, with few needs, who remember God and are blessed."

"You are right," admitted Mian Mitha, "but what is the origin of suffering?"

"The root of suffering is evil—the greed of self which burns like an unquenched fire—the more it is fed the stronger its flames rise. One says this world is a place of suffering, dominated by desire. One cannot give it up and so the root of suffering remains and men die like flies in search of the sweets of life. They who by God's grace overcome desire, cross the troubled sea of suffering."

"Tell me," asked the Sufi, "how does a person become fit to enter the Court of God?"

"The facade of illusion cannot be penetrated," said Nanak, "nor can any weapon cleave it. The only way to escape from it is to submit to the will of God. Then the greedy mind turns back from the objects of desire."

Mian Mitha then asked, "How can a lamp be lighted without oil?"—meaning that without the aid of a holy book like the Koran, how could one be illuminated?

"Make fear of the Lord the wick and light it up with discrimination between the real and the unreal. The lamp will burn without oil and in its light, the Lord Himself will be seen."

"How can one have a clean slate at the end of His life?"

"This world is a place of coming and going and when one is called to account, release will be the reward of true service. Therefore, serve His creation with all your might. To gain admission to His presence, unload the burden of actions, which form the cause and create Karma."

"What you say is true," said Mian Mitha. "I feel as if I have not been acting on what the Holy Book teaches. I have not dedicated my life to service of God and His creation, but now tell me the hidden power of the sacred Name."

"Close your eyes," instructed the Guru. He said "La" and as he uttered the Word, the whole creation disappeared. Then he uttered "Allah" and the creation came into existence again.

Mian Mitha opened his eyes, bewildered by the power of the Word.

"Know," said the Guru, "that the Word brought the universe into existence and the Word can gather it back again."

 ## THE ETERNAL BRIDE

The Guru proceeded to a neighboring town where a fair was taking place in honor of a Fakir, who called himself the "Eternal Bride." It was said that this was the day when he saw his Beloved and people came from long distances to see him. Nanak walked up to his house but was refused admission. The doorkeeper said, "He is in communion with the Beloved."

The Guru laughed and said, "I must lift the curtain."

"What do you mean?" called the crowd which gathered round him.

"Go and see," said the Guru, "who he is in communion with."

The crowd received this as a command, pushed past the doorkeeper and entered the sanctuary. They found the Fakir in bed with some women who had come to worship him and had been specially admitted.

The Guru, meanwhile, retired to a mango grove close by. He was sitting filled with joy, when a crippled beggar dragged himself up to touch his feet. The Guru looked at the cripple compassionately, uttered Sat Nam and sprinkled some water on him. The man dropped his crutches and walked as if he had never been crippled. He walked back to the town and the news spread all around.

Meanwhile, the "Eternal Bride" was being pursued by the angry crowd. The crowd had dismantled his banners and drums and broken his doors. In despair he ran to the Guru for protection, and fell at his feet saying, "Save me and teach me."

The crowd fell back at the Guru's command.

"Sit down," he said to the Fakir. "I unveiled you with no other purpose than to put you on the right path."

"How can I know it, teacher?" asked the Fakir.

"You must not deceive people anymore. Make your heart pure and see Him, not in any particular form, but in all that exists. The Beloved resides in you and in all that there is. It is not by wearing bridal garments that the bridegroom is won. You who claim to be the bride of Him who never dies, you must know that you cannot deceive the All-Seeing, who knows our inner-most thoughts. It is by following truth that you can gain honor. The world reveres those who follow the right path."

"Bless my house with your presence," pleaded the 'Eternal Bride,' "and teach me the way."

"Will you promise to give up this false show and do as I tell you?"

"I will obey you, my master," he answered.

Nanak then walked to his house, now crowded with eager pilgrims.

"Listen," said the Guru:

> Foolish one, why are you self-satisfied?
> Why do you not enjoy the Beloved in your own house?
> The Beloved is within you, why do you seek him outside?
> Adorn your eyes with the eye-shadow of His fear
> And imbue yourself with the adornment of love.
> If He looks at you with favor
> Then indeed you would become a bride.

"How can I win His love?" asked the 'Eternal Bride'. "How can I become acceptable?"

"You ask me," said the Guru, "what is a young and ignorant person to do, if she fails to win His love, in spite of all her efforts, her grief and her tears? I must tell you, howsoever one may try, without right action nothing is gained. How can she win her Lord when the darkness of desire and greed and the delusion of Maya possess her mind. As long as they prevail the Beloved cannot be found."

"Then how can He be found?" asked the Fakir.

"Get rid of those enemies and then go and ask those who have won His favor, by what means they have won the Beloved. They will tell you. Learn to abide by His will and accept what comes with gladness, wisely carrying out His command. Fix your mind on the feet of Him whose love is everlasting. Whatever He says must be obeyed, and mind and body consecrated to His service. It is thus, that the Beloved can be found."

"Tell me more about it," he said. "My mind is slowly clearing."

"Listen," said the Guru. "It is by losing the self that God is found; cleverness is of no use. The day He looks at you with favor, only that day counts, for it is then that all the longings of the soul are fulfilled. She who is loved by her bridegroom is indeed blessed. She is exalted, imbued with the love of her Lord, absorbed in His love, day and night. Such a one, beautiful beyond compare, is indeed truly wise."

"What is love?" asked the Fakir. "Some people call passion love."

"Love," said the Guru, "cannot be defined in words. It can only be experienced. It is an act of complete self-surrender, an act of inner consecration, which is beyond human power to control. When we love God, we find Him in the temple of our heart and in the heart of all that lives and thus, in loving Him, we love all that exists."

The crowd sat spell-bound listening to the Guru and basking in the light which radiated from his words. Soon after, the Guru returned home to Kartarpur.

 THE SACRED WORD

Seekers of truth of all denominations came to Kartarpur from long distances to ask questions.

"We are told by you to remember God and to serve Him," asked a disciple of the Guru, "but how can we do so? We repeat the Word but only our lips move. Our hearts are not freed from self-seeking."

"It is only through His favor that the power to remember Him is gained," said the Guru. "Then the heart melts, selfish motives die within us, the lower self becomes one with the higher self. By the kindness of the Guru, the mind is linked with God. Death does not destroy Him.

"Acquire the wings of virtue in the days that are given to you. Lead a harmless and righteous life. Righteousness opens the gateway to realization. Replace lust, wrath, covetousness and evil thought by dispassion, desirelessness, forgiveness and love. In this way remove the evil that clouds the consciousness and discover the difference between the real and unreal. Then control the mind and allow it to wander no more. God's first manifestation was sound. It is from sound that the whole universe flowed forth. Therefore the sacred Word is the only manifestation of God. Charge every breath with the sacred Word."

"Tell us what that Word is," asked another.

"The unmanifested," said the Guru, "manifests Himself in sound—Shabad—and from Shabad the whole creation flows forth. Shabad, therefore, represents Him in this world. The way to Him is through the Shabad."

> The Brahma, the creator,
> Was created by Ong Kar.*
> From the Word Om again,
> Came the universal mind.
> From the Word came forth time
> And the limit of ages.
> From the Word came the Vedas.
> Salvation is found
> In the Word Om.
> The righteous disciple
> Crosses the ocean by it.
> Meditate on the Word Om—
> In the Word Om
> Is the knowledge of the three worlds.

MECCA — THE KAABA

After a long stay at Kartarpur, the Guru once again started his travels. This time he chose to visit the Muslim lands of the Middle East. Wearing a long yellow robe and carrying the staff of a Muslim pilgrim, he set off for Mecca accompanied by his companions: Bala, a Hindu, and Mardana, a Muslim. He carried with him a Koran and a prayer-mat. Whenever the occasion arose he performed his prayers in the Muslim manner so as not to arouse the suspicions of those who might prevent him from making the sacred journey, permissable only to Muslims.

The Guru joined up with a group of fakirs. After a few days of traveling together one asked him what his religion was.

"I belong to the religion of those who follow the path of God," replied Nanak.

* Om before Kar becomes Ong Kar. Om is the absolute self of the Creator. Ong is the creative self of the Creator.

56

They pressed him to confess that he was a Muslim but he refused to do so. This greatly troubled them. They were not sure whether they were right in having along a man who was an infidel. The Guru saw this and disappeared with his two attendants. They noticed that a cloud that had protected them from the scorching rays of the sun also disappeared with him.

The fakirs thought that traveling by himself in the desert he would never reach Mecca. They were astonished when they found that the Guru had already arrived with his two attendants. They were even more puzzled when they were told that the Guru had been there for several days. They were convinced that he was some great soul and begged him to forgive them for their suspicions about him.

The keeper of the Kaaba—a sacred building in Mecca—one night discovered that the Guru was sleeping with his feet towards the Kaaba. It was time for prayer so he informed the priest that a pilgrim was committing a great sacrilege by turning his feet towards the house of God. The incensed priest rushed to where the Guru was sleeping.

"Wake up, you stupid fool," he screamed, "and rub your face on the ground and beg to be forgiven for turning your feet towards the house of God."

The Guru did not move, but quietly said, "Turn my feet towards the place where God does not dwell."

The priest could no longer control himself and ordered the keeper to take Nanak by the feet and turn him around in the other direction. The door keeper obeyed but whichever direction they turned his feet the Kaaba turned with them. The priest stood spell-bound. He saw that the house of God was in all directions.

The Guru rose and looked at the priest with eyes full of compassion. "Your eyes have been opened for just a moment," he said. "Don't forget what you have seen. All space is nothing but God's dwelling place."

The priest bowed before the Guru, then went to tell his Chief, Rukin-ud-Din, the High Priest, what had happened. The Chief, a seeker after truth, hastened to the Guru hopeful of getting a glimpse of his eternal light. He saluted respectfully. The Guru returned the salute, and then he sat down beside him.

"You are a godly man from all appearance," said the High Priest, "but tell me to what religion you belong."

"I believe in the religion of Him, who is the master of all that is visible and invisible," answered the Guru.

"What do you mean by Him?" asked Rukin-ud-Din.

"He who is without a second," said the Guru, "to whom birth and death are not known. Who is beyond all change, and who pervades everywhere—lands, seas and skies."

"So you believe in one God. You must be a Muslim."

"I accept no creed," said the Guru. "I am His slave and slaves have not even their own will. How can they who yield unwavering obedience to the Lord accept any creed?"

"God as you have described Him is the same God of which our Kalma in the Koran speaks," repeated Rukin-ud-Din. "Why not acknowledge yourself to be a Muslim?"

"The Vedas too speak of one God, the supreme God of all," Nanak said. "Then why should not I declare myself a Hindu? Truth remains Truth. It is the colored lenses of the self that reflect it in various colors. A servant of God, aware of His presence, cannot accept creeds, which imprison truth and impose on it their own limitations."

"How do you make this out?" asked Rukin-ud-Din.

"You have an example before your eyes. You call this sacred temple a house of God. If you were a true believer, you would find that there is no place where the house of God does not exist. Further, you say you believe in one God. Then why don't you recognize in men of diverse creeds a brother? If this truth dwelt in your heart, you would act in its light. You would not believe that kissing a black stone was the highest religious act."

The High Priest was much impressed and said, "Come and join us tomorrow in the ceremony of sacrifice. I will provide a camel for you."

"Why?" the Guru laughed.

"God is pleased with sacrifices," replied Rukin-ud-Din. "He bestows His mercy on those who offer a sacrifice."

"If a drop of blood pollutes your garments," said the Guru, "how can the spilling of blood be pleasing to God?"

"I do not know," said Rukin-ud-Din, "but sacrifice is prescribed by Shariat—the sacred law of the Muslims. To follow the law is the best of acts."

"The law of love ordains that one should be harmless in thought and act," said the Guru. "Treat others as you would have them treat you. Righteousness is the unalterable law of living for all people."

"If you follow no written law, what about giving justice to others?"

"If we live justly, the need for administering justice does not arise. If we forgive those who harm us, we need invoke no man-made law. If we live as members of one human family, every individual living for the other, then we follow the divine law and if we follow the divine law we transform this world full of misery into a world of happiness. In such a kingdom there is no need of any law and for any administrators of law. It is because we fail to follow the Divine Law that we submit to man-made law to rectify the self-aggrandisement of men."

"How are sinners to be punished if we do not follow the Shariat?" asked the High Priest. "Tell me what is your conception of sin?"

"We sin," said the Guru, "when we fail to follow the divine law of love. We sin when we trespass on the rights of others for our own selfish ends, when we cause them injury. In short, to do harm is to sin."

"Such acts as do no harm to anyone and yet have their root in self, are they not sinful?"

"God reads hearts. He sees what passes in our minds. Unselfish acts partake of the spirit of sacrifice and such acts are blessed, while selfish acts bring pain and suffering."

"What do you mean by sacrifice?" asked Rukin-ud-Din. "You refused to sacrifice when I invited you to do so."

"My good friend, we sacrifice when we deprive the self of what it holds dear, to serve others or to serve a good cause. To kill a sheep and feast on its flesh is no sacrifice," answered the Guru. "To give what one needs for one's self to another, whose need is greater, is an act of sacrifice. They who give and expect a return make no sacrifice. They are like a money-lender who makes advances at compound interest. They who give and want nothing in return are the real givers, but he who takes all he can without giving is below the human stage. The dead body of an animal and its bones are of some use, but the dead body of a man requires a plot of earth to be buried in or fuel for cremation. He who gives in the hope of a return is human, he who gives without any wish for a reward is divine."

"Instruct me in the art of true living," begged the High Priest.

"Let your heart and mind put on the garb of a pilgrim. Every hour of the night and day seek your Maker. Rub out from the tablet of the mind all that is written there and polish it into the brightness of a mirror. There will then appear on it a luminous spark. This spark will become the sun and a soundless sound will fill your heart with divine music and draw you near to God."

 ## THE GRAND MUFTI OF BAGHDAD

From Mecca the Guru proceeded to Medina and from Medina to the great city of Baghdad. He reached there about nightfall and stopped outside the town at a place where lepers were segregated with no provision for their comfort or treatment.

They crowded round the Guru crying loudly. Nanak was moved and asked them to pass before him one by one. He took some water and sprinkled it on the leper who came before him and he walked away entirely cured. The lepers that were healed ran to the city next morning and spread the news of their healing. The people from the city came in crowds to see the miracle worker.

"Listen, my people," said the Guru, addressing them, "I have worked no miracle. Mercy is of God and He acts through those who are instruments of His will. He is known as Rahim, the Merciful. He is known as Karim, the Giver, and yet we seek other doors than His."

The Grand Mufti of the city sent a messenger to ask the Guru to come to him.

Nanak said, "I stay where I like. I go where I like. If the Mufti wishes to see me he can come here."

The Mufti, when he received the message, went in all his pomp to see the Guru.

"I want to discuss things with you," he began.

"Discussion is like the wind that blows," said the Guru, "unless there is a spark of fire in the heart which can be blown into the fire of devotion."

"What do you mean?" asked the Mufti.

"I mean," said the Guru, "that discussion is only fruitful if it lights the hidden fire of devotion."

"Do you know the Kalma?" asked the Mufti, to change the subject.

"May I repeat the question?" asked the Guru. "Do you know it?"

The Mufti laughed with scorn. "I am a Muslim. How can you ask me this foolish question?"

"I asked the question, because I am sure your tongue recites the Kalma, but it passes over your heart as water over a stone."

"The Kalma is my life-breath," protested the Mufti. "What do you mean?"

"Didn't I say that discussion is mere wind?" said the Guru. "You may recite the Kalma loudly but it doesn't reach your heart, which is full of other needs."

"What is that?" asked the Mufti.

"You begin by saying that there is no other God but Allah, and yet you call men of other religions infidels. They are also of the one God, who has no second. You repeat the Kalma and yet your heart is not moved with forgiveness, nor your hand moved to give. You love other things better than the one God you invoke. My friend, do you not realize that you render lip service to Allah, while you worship other objects. Allah is on your tongue and that which is other than Allah possesses your heart."

As the two men talked a man came running and fell at the Guru's feet. "Protect me, great one," he begged.

"Tell me who is persecuting you," asked the Guru.

He looked at the Mufti and trembled, "I have been condemned to be stoned to death."

"I remember," said the Mufti, "this man has committed a serious crime. He has been sentenced to be stoned to death according to that Shariat. He deserves no consideration whatsoever."

"Ah," said the Guru, "remember the Kalma. God is merciful. God is all-forgiving. We act as God would wish us to act, when we show mercy, when we forgive even our enemies. Do those who administer law in their own person break no law? The laws of the holy Koran, no, of God Himself, pray for forgiveness. God is merciful. He will forgive you. God commands you to show mercy to this man."

The Mufti felt as if commanded by God himself. "I'll obey you, great one," he said.

The Guru then instructed the Mufti in the art of right living and discovering the way to God, and, after a few days' stay left Baghdad.

SUFIS

Some time later the Guru was passing through Persia and was near Tehran when he came upon a center of Sufis. They welcomed him and invited him to occupy a seat near their leader, who offered him food and drink.

"From where have you come?" asked the senior Sufi. "And what is your destination?"

"I come from everywhere into here and I must return from here into everywhere."

"Have you brought any news of the Beloved?"

"Doesn't the heart talk of Him all the time with the rhythm of its beat? Don't we receive news of the Beloved with every ingoing and outgoing breath?

"Why is there such ignorance about Him then?" asked the Sufi.

"As light is located in darkness," answered the Guru.

"Why does the sun set?" asked the Sufi.

"The sun never sets. It is just a dot that makes day and night."

"Where is light to be found?" asked the Sufi.

"In the darkness itself," answered the Guru. "The dawn of the morning is hidden in the gloom of the night."

"What is the secret of darkness and light?" asked the Sufi.

"There is none," said the Guru. "Both are the same. There is darkness in light and light in darkness. To lose the self is to become light. To assert the self is to become darkness. Self-assertion freezes the self into darkness. The fire of love melts the self into light."

"The blessings of God be on you," said the Sufi. "You indeed are a knower."

Next the Guru stopped in a village where a Fakir came to him and said, "My Pir has sent me to request you to visit him. He is most anxious to meet you."

"How did he know that I was here?" asked the Guru.

"My Pir is endowed with the light of the spirit," answered the Fakir.

The Guru smiled and accompanied the Fakir to his master, who came forward to receive him and conducted him to his simple home.

The Guru stayed with him for a few days. The leader of the Sufis enjoyed the company of the Guru, while his disciples asked the Guru to solve their problems.

One of them one day asked, "Tell me something about the 'Friend'."

"How can I describe Him?" said the Guru. "How can the tongue speak about Him, who is the speech of the tongue?"

"Why has the world been created?" asked the disciple.

"To experience its futility and to discard it," replied the Guru.

"What is the object of creation?" inquired the disciple.

"The body is created only to die. It is the garment of the spirit, which must rise out of its imprisoned self into freedom."

"How can this be achieved?" he was asked again.

"There is no other way," said the Guru, "but to surrender the self to the Beloved and find satisfaction in what he ordains pleasant or painful."

"How can we find the way of life in the darkness of the world?"

"Make yourself the instrument of His will and serve His creation. Actions thus performed feed the sacrificial fire and leave no trace behind. In this way the shadows of separation and hate are dispersed, the gates of love and union flung wide open, and the Lord and His devotee become one."

"If there is no other but Him," asked the Sufi, "what is the meaning of union?"

"This mystery no words can explain. It is only resolved when God is realized."

"What prevents our realizing God?"

"The shadow of selfhood," said the Guru. "The awareness of the separate self and the desire for things which haunts the separated self."

"How can this shadow be dispersed?" asked the disciple.

"By invoking his Sacred Name and purifying the mind and intellect of all impurities."

"What is the Sacred Name?"

"People call Him by various names, but the whole Universe

manifested itself from the sound of the Sacred Name. It is the life of all life."

"By whatever name men call Him, it is Him the one God they remember. Then why is there such antagonism between the Hindus and Muslims?"

"Ignorance is the cause of all religious conflicts. People talk and yet fail to realize religion. There is no difference between Hindu and Muslim. Both are from the same mold. Only the veil of ignorance separates them."

"What is the cause of ignorance?"

"You ask questions," said the Guru, "as if words can dispel the darkness of the mind. Ignorance has its roots in the ego, it does not see Him in all things, but makes Him an image of itself. God alone is true, He is unchanging, all else is untrue. He is beyond life and death, fear, attachment and hate. His Name is true."

The disciple, greatly impressed, kissed the hands of the Guru and said, "You are indeed a messenger of God. The light of God is in all that you utter."

 ## THIS SOUL IS LIKE A FISH

The Guru visited Dayalpur and stayed with a poor peasant who was his disciple. He had not been there long, when he was disturbed by the sound of loud crying coming from a neighboring house. The heart-rending cries touched his heart and he asked why the neighbor was so grief-stricken.

"She is a poor woman," said his host. "Her only son, who is her sole support was run over by a wheel of a bullock cart and broke his leg. He has been in great pain ever since and unable to work."

The Guru, moved with pity, got up and walked to the adjoining hut.

The old woman, seeing the Guru entering, fell at his feet. "Maharaj, save my son," she pleaded. "We have been staying alive by dissolving ashes in water and drinking the mixture. No one has come to our help. My son, the prop of my old age, see, he is huddled up with a a broken leg and a fever that never leaves him." She again broke into sobs.

The Guru, compassion incarnate, approached the sick man and looked at him with eyes full of the nectar of healing. He took a little water, uttered Sat Nam and sprinkled it on the man and commanded, "You are healed, rise."

The man threw off his rags nervously, straightened himself and stood up. He could hardly believe that he was healed.

The mother was overjoyed to see her son completely recovered.

She passed her hand over his broken leg and then she clasped the feet of the Guru, full of deep gratitude. "You have saved my life, you have saved my son."

"God is all-merciful," said the Guru, "and His grace is always with those who in full faith seek it and turn to Him for protection."

The Guru turned to the young man and asked, "How do you earn your living?"

"I am a fisherman," replied the young man. "I catch fish and then sell them in the bazaar and with the money that I get I purchase our daily needs. I earn just enough to keep body and soul together and to serve the meager needs of my mother."

The Guru said, "This soul is like a fish, led into the net of the fisherman, Death, by desire. The mind, unconscious of truth, falls into the whirlpool of unending cares. The mind urged on by hunger does not realize the danger and walks into the net. He himself shows the way of union to whom he accepts."

The well-to-do neighbor of the fisherman walked in and asked, "What should a man do to obtain salvation?"

"My brother, one must love all beings, but to reach that stage one has to make a beginning. If you cannot love your neighbor, how can you love those who are strangers? When your neighbor was in pain, how could you eat bread quietly and sleep comfortably?"

In the meantime news of the miracle spread and the whole village came to receive the Guru's blessings.

THE MOGHUL EMPEROR BABAR

A vision came to Guru Nanak that Sayadpur was to be invaded and plundered by the Moghul emperor Babar and so he returned there to save his devotee, Lalo.

A few days later, as if from out of nowhere, Babar arrived with his army, sacked the town and subjected it to massacre, looting and rape. The Guru with Bala and Mardana was captured and made to carry the loot with the other prisoners. As they walked, the loads on the heads of the Guru and Bala were seen to rise up a foot above their heads, and were carried by the air. The horse Mardana was given to lead followed him of its own free will.

The prisoners were taken to a camp where both men and women were made to grind corn at hand-worked stonemills. The Guru, when required to do so, went into Samadhi and his grinding mill worked by itself. Those who observed the incredible sight carried the news to Babar.

Babar would not believe it and came to see the Guru himself. He stood spell-bound as he saw the mill working. He waited until the Guru opened his eyes and then with folded hands bowed to him and begged to be forgiven. Babar then invited the Guru to accompany him to his tent. He agreed and when they arrived the Emperor offered him a cup of wine.

The Guru smiled and said, "I take no intoxicants which cloud the mind for a little while and leave one cold and frustrated. I'm inebriated with something more enduring than this." Babar misunderstood him, and offered him some hashish instead. The Guru, much amused, sang the following hymn to explain himself:

> Love is my hemp, my heart its pouch.
> O God, I am mad for you, aloof from the rest.
> With prayerful hands as the bowl, it is for the
> Vision of You I beg at Your door.

"Listen, O King," said the Guru, "look around you. Take a warning from those whom you have defeated. Victory and defeat come from God. Do not forget that he who is victorious today may suffer the fate of the defeated tomorrow if he fails to glorify God. They who ruled here yesterday, where are they today?"

Babar remained deep in thought for a long while and then said, "You believe in one God. My religion also teaches what you teach. Embrace Islam, then; on the day of judgment, the Prophet himself will intercede for you."

"O King," said the Guru, "at the gate of the Lord many messengers stand waiting. There are hundreds of thousands of Mohammads at His Court. Their number cannot be counted. They are sent at His bidding. He sends prophets into the world and recalls them at His will. I know that only God is pure and perfect. All else is impure and imperfect."

Babar was greatly impressed and asked, "What can I do for you?"

"Nothing," said the Guru. "It is the one God Who has commissioned me and I enjoy His gifts. To depend on human beings and not on Him is to lose both the worlds. The giver is One, the whole world begs at His door. They who forsake Him and attach themselves to others lose all. He makes emperors and kings. No one is His equal. Hear, Emperor Babar, he who begs from you is a fool."

"True teacher," said Babar, "I beg of you to give me a gift, for you are a representative of God."

"Ask, Babar," the Guru answered.

"Give me the throne of Delhi in perpetuity," asked Babar.

"Nothing in this transitory world is permanent," said the Guru. "But your successors will rule for many generations."

"You have bestowed on me the kingdom of the earth. Teach me how to enter heaven."

"Be just and never do that which is unjust," said the Guru. "Never depart from the path of truth. Temper justice with mercy, and forgive others as you wish to be forgiven. Do not covet that which is meant for others, for God is just. Do not act when you are burning with any of the five fires. Always act for the benefit of others. Do not sow the seed of cruelty. He who is cruel, himself suffers cruelty."

The Guru then took leave of Babar and led Lalo back to his home which had been saved by the grace of the Guru.

THE WELL, THE WALI AND THE BOULDER

On a hill near Hasan Abdal in the Punjab lived a Muslim Fakir known as Wali Kandhari. He had a great following of disciples and was said to possess supernatural powers. By the side of a natural spring he had built a house and sanctuary in which he was said to hold communion with God. The spring fed a well which he owned. There was no other water in the immediate area. It was at this place that the Guru and his two companions came to stop.

Mardana was feeling thirsty and the Guru told him to go to the top of the hill and quench his thirst from the well. He climbed up and as he approached the well, saw the Wali sitting near it and respectfully bowed.

"Why have you come here?" inquired the Wali.

"I am a servant of Guru Nanak, who is a holy person," Mardana replied. "He is sitting below the hill. I am thirsty. I asked the Guru to tell me where to get water and he directed me to come to you."

The Wali was annoyed to hear of another holy man coming to the place and not paying him homage.

"Get out," he said. "If your master is a holy man, why doesn't he get water for you instead of sending you to me? I cannot allow you to take water from my well."

Poor Mardana returned disappointed and told the Guru what had happened.

"Never mind what the Wali said. Go back and ask for water again with all humility," commanded the Guru.

Mardana was tired and thirsty but he could not disobey his master, so he made another attempt and went up the hill and again begged humbly for water.

The Wali shouted, "Go back. Tell your master to produce water for you to drink."

Mardana came back to the Guru tired and thirsty and almost fainting.

The Guru smiled and said, "Mardana, utter Sat Nam and dig a little hole where you are sitting." Mardana did as he was ordered. Immediately water spouted up and began to flow.

The Wali who was still sitting at his well observed that it was getting drained.

Mardana quenched his thirst and sat quietly near his master. The Wali was deeply concerned as his well began to get empty. He got up and saw the water flowing at the feet of the Guru. His rage knew no bounds. There was a big boulder lying near him. He rolled it down so that it would fall on the Guru and crush him.

Bala saw the boulder thundering down and warned his master. The Guru did not move but at the last moment raised his hand to stop it. It stopped dead and received the imprint of the Guru's hand on it.

The Wali was frightened and humbly came down and bowed before the Guru, who received him and asked him to sit down. The Wali sat down and asked the Guru, "Tell me how did you acquire this power?"

"My dear Wali," said the Guru, "power belongs to the All-powerful. Human beings are powerless. It is only when we take shelter in Him that He extends His protecting hand. There is no power higher than truth. That which is false cannot endure. It must fail in the end.

> Listen to true advice
> Your record will be taken out
> And you will be called to render an account.
> Those whose account is not clear
> Will have to face an urgent demand.
> The angel of death will hold them.
> From that narrow lane there will be no escape.
> The false will fail,
> Only the Truth shall prevail.

The Wali was deeply impressed. "The Holy Prophet has said, 'Learn to die while living.' How can this be done? How can we realize that all is His, and which is the best name of God?"

"If the self dies when we are living, we follow the way of the Prophet. It is only with the death of the separating self that we realize all is His. By whatever name we remember Him it is the best."

The Wali then asked him to come with him to the sanctuary.

"It is difficult to enter the gate of His house and occupy the holy place. I am happy where I am."

They spent a great deal of time together talking of things of the spirit.

67

In the beautiful valley of Kashmir crowds gathered round the Guru to receive his teaching wherever he went. He reached Srinagar where a very learned Pandit by the name of Brahm Dass lived who was said to have acquired supernatural powers and was a devotee of the goddess. The news that a great teacher had arrived reached him and he decided to visit the Guru.

It was said that he made the carpet on which he sat fly into the air, so that he might impress and dazzle the Guru by the display of his powers. When he reached the place, he saw that a large crowd was sitting there, but he could not see the Guru so inquired, "Where is the Guru?"

"He is sitting just in front of you," they replied.

"Why can't I see him?" he asked.

"How can we tell?" they replied. "He is right in front of you."

The Pandit was not only annoyed but felt humiliated as his carpet refused to fly back to his place. He had no option but to walk back deeply hurt.

He sat brooding over the incident, when one of his disciples came to see him. "You have all deceived me," he said. "There was no Guru present, otherwise why could I not see him?"

"He was there," asserted the disciple. "It was your pride that darkened your vision. If you go on foot without pride of power, you will benefit by the sight of him."

The Pandit next day waited in all humility on the Guru and with folded hands he fell at his feet. The Guru received him very cordially and asked him to sit beside him.

Then the Pandit asked the Guru, "First of all, please tell me why I could not see you yesterday."

"How could you see me in extreme darkness?"

"But it was broad daylight."

"Is there any darkness denser than pride?" asked the Guru. "Because you could fly you thought you were almost a superman. Birds and insects fly in the air. Are they of any account?"

The truth struck home. "Forgive me, teacher," he exclaimed. "I have read sacred books and acquired superphysical powers. I must confess I have found no peace. Tell me how I can touch the feet of the Lord."

"Knowledge which partakes of the darkness of the ego is of little avail," said the Guru.

Brahm Dass again fell at the feet of the Guru and exclaimed, "Great Guru, I was mistaken, save me. My time is short."

He had an idol of Shiva tied with a string round his neck, and he removed it there and then.

The Guru said, "You have worshipped other gods, who perish like men. You have followed men of much learning, but you have not grasped the truth that is within you. You have sought Him in things which are a mere reflection of reality. You are lost in the wilderness of knowledge. Words only acquire a meaning when you realize the truth of which they are the symbols."

The Guru sang this hymn while Mardana played on the Rubab.

> Another man's wife, another man's property,
> Covetousness, evil desire, search of sense objects,
> Bad temper, backbiting, lustfulness and wrath—
> He who rids himself of these
> Will find in himself the Infinite, the Unknowable.
> This hidden nectar only he discovers
> Who receives the jewel of the Guru's Word
> And makes it his life breath.
> He is not disturbed by pleasure or pain.
> Good and evil they are all the same to Him.
> In the dawn of true wisdom—buddhi—
> Fed by the light of God's Name,
> In the company of saints, devoted to the Guru,
> The Guru, the Giver, bestows the sacred Name.
> Treasuring it, the disciple is absorbed in Him.
> He alone obtains the sacred Word
> Who earns the grace of the Lord.
> This body is the temple of the Lord.
> In the heart is his light.
> Says Nanak, let the Word of the Guru
> Enter the heart and by the grace of God
> Effect everlasting union.

The Pandit bowed and said, "I have now learned the truth, to seek within and not outside, to get rid of the evil passions, to seek the favor of the Lord and remain absorbed in the Guru's Word."

   IN TIBET – THE LAMA AND THE ABSOLUTE

From Srinagar the Guru traveled into lower Tibet and approached a monastery. The Head Lama came to meet him and welcomed him to his monastic home. He offered the Guru refreshment, made him comfortable and then quietly inquired, "They say there are many creeds prevalent down in the plains and the learned expound many philosophies. What do you say about the creation of this world and the Creator?"

The Guru said:

> From the soundless Absolute proceeds everything.
> He, the soundless, emanates sound
> And from it flows forth air, water, fire, light, and souls.
> He, the Absolute, remains unaffected
> And yet maintains all that lives.
> He, the Lord of creation, rejoices in his own creation.
> The Absolute produces Brahma, Vishnu, Shiva
> And also time and the four great ages.
> He who knows the Absolute as all-pervading
> Is a perfect man, and in his company delusion is destroyed.

The Lama heaved a deep sigh. "I have heard before the theory of the Absolute and your definition has cleared it up a good deal. Tell me more about it."

"The Absolute produces heaven and earth and without any support maintains them. The three worlds come forth from the Absolute and are permeated with the Maya of the Absolute. They are its manifestations and are absorbed in it. From the Absolute arise differentiations, the species and all the four forms of speech. They are absorbed in it again. From it also arise the seven regions and the fourteen spheres. They are all its creation, caused by it, and to be absorbed in it. From the Absolute proceed day and night, that measures out pleasure and pain. It is by constant search that we find the way to cross the bounds of time, and become immortal. It is thus that righteous seekers find their heaven.

"From the Absolute are radiated sun and moon. The light of the Absolute pervades the three worlds. The Absolute is limitless and indescribable. The Absolute is Samadhi itself. The source of the seven seas is the Absolute and also all knowledge. When the human mind, by the power of the Word communicated by the Guru, bathes in the lake of Truth, it obtains release from the wheel of birth and death."

The Lama smiled and said, "So the Truth of the Lord Buddha still remains that all beings are tied to the wheel and suffer agonies till they obtain release by following the eight-fold path."

"Yes," said the Guru, "the Absolute manifests itself as God, his incarnations are the Avatars. He makes gods, demi-gods, elemental and celestial music-makers, ordained to perform their various duties. He produces the three Gunas—the basic tendencies—Tamasic, Rajasic and Sattvic: of inertia, energy and pure spirit. These are shadows of His manifestations. The spirit imprisoned in the five elements sows the seeds of acts, good and bad, merit and demerit. One's own deeds make the destiny which is inscribed on the forehead of everyone and brings the harvest of one's own sowing through cycles of births and deaths. By Divine grace, when the true teacher imparts the Word, the Turia stage is attained, with it the divine consciousness, and with it the gift of freedom from the domination of Gunas."

"This too I have heard," said the Lama, "also the great books of knowledge teach the same truth. I like to hear from you, for your words are like shafts of light, which illumine the darkness of the mind."

"The Sam, Rig, Yajur and Atharva Vedas which Brahma is constantly reciting and to which you have referred are books of knowledge. They and even Maya, with its three attributes—Gunas—come from the Absolute. Limited power of expression comes from the Absolute, so no one can describe the Absolute. What we must learn is the cure of suffering which humanity inherits. Suffering ceases when the Word of the teacher enters the heart. Only a rare one reaches this stage and receives the gift of emancipation, such a one is emancipated for all time. He is perfect. He is exalted."

"What are the attributes of a true teacher?" inquired the Lama, who was deeply interested and was trying to test the truth of the Guru's teachings in the light of his knowledge of the gospel of Buddha.

"The true teacher is intoxicated with the love of God. He is one with God. He is unique. He is exalted, wisdom and power are his gifts. When good fortune favors, a Guru is met. Mind is no more attached to worldly objects. He destroys delusions."

"Can a philosopher break the bonds of attachment?"

"No, it is only the true teacher who awakens the Buddhi, supreme wisdom, and opens the door that leads to the Guru," said Nanak. "Then the pure sound of the true Word is heard and the true Name of the Lord enters the heart and samadhi is attained."

The Lama was very pleased and asked, "How can we reach the Absolute?"

"The Absolute is in you," said the Guru. "Its light is in every heart. It is only discovered under the instructions of the true teacher. The Absolute is all that is. All is in one and the one is in all. This secret is revealed by the Guru. This secret is known when you know yourself and realize yourself in all beings. He is exalted who recognizes himself in all beings."

"Tell me what stands in the way of righteousness?" asked the Lama. "Where is the mind situated? How can it become an abode of peace? Show me the way from the unreal to the real."

"Five passions rooted in desire possess the mind, and these lead the mind astray. It wanders after objects of desire unaware of the inner peace. The mind is in the body. It is the mirror of the True One. It is obscured by desire, but when it is disassociated from the search of that which is false and transitory it finds peace in the True One.

71

The way from the unreal to the real is discovered by purification of the self, by performance of righteous acts and constant striving for spiritual advancement. He who is not truthful, he whose life is unrighteous, cannot understand the meaning of Mukti or Salvation. He who approaches the Primal Being after self-purification attains with ease the union. He is freed from births and deaths, coming and going. He, the devotee of the Lord, becomes established in the Lord. Nothing else exists for him"

"You said that the Absolute is Infinite. How can a finite being become one with the Infinite?"

"Just as the tree and its fruit are the same," said the Guru. "They who eat the fruit of the tree of immortality and drink its nectar become one with the Supreme. He who knows the self becomes one with the Supreme Self."

"Why does pain haunt those who work for pleasure?" asked the Lama.

"Pain is but the reflex of pleasure. When we seek pleasure, we also court pain. The only way to escape pain is to quench the thirst for pleasure, and remain unaffected by both pleasure and pain. Everyone is eager to secure pleasure. No one desires pain. The ignorant see not the truth that pain follows pleasure. When pleasure and pain become the same, and these two impostors are defeated, the secret Word opens the door of true bliss."

THE LAND OF PERPETUAL SNOWS

There was going to be a great gathering of saints and sages and masters of wisdom at Lake Mansarowar—the Sacred Lake of the Gods. The Lama asked whether the Guru would like to go there.

"It is for Mansarowar that I am bound," said the Guru.

In due time the Guru and the Lama left the monastery and traveled to the land of perpetual snows, shining in its purity like a sea of glass. There he met the great ascetics, the renouncers of the world and saints with supernatural powers."

"How is India faring?" they asked him.

"Why do you ask me?" he said. "You know that the dark age is like a knife, which kings handle like butchers. Justice has taken wing and flown away. The darkness of untruth obscures even the light of the moon, which cannot be seen. I am perplexed at how to show you the true way in this dreary darkness. Humanity is groaning under the dread domination of the self, and yet falsehood must fail, and truth prevail."

"Hail, hail, Nanak," they called, "His light will prevail." The Guru answered, "Hail, hail to Him, the Lord of all."

Then he passed into a trance and sang the following hymn:

He is the True One
There is no other.
He sends forth the Universe
And absorbs it in Himself
As it pleases Him.
He keeps us.
He cannot be questioned.

He is the Creator of the three gunas.
He drives us to action and bondage,
And Himself shows the way of freedom
He Himself is all-wisdom,
He Himself is the knower,
He Himself is ever satisfied.

He is air, water and fire,
He is the sun and the moon,
He is knowledge and meditation,
He is the true teacher.
They are not enmeshed
In the net of time
Who take refuge in the True One.

He is the male, He is the female
He is the dice, He is the pawn
He is the play, He is the player
He is the day, He is the night
He is the primal being, beginningless, soundless
Dwelling everywhere, the Lord of the world.
He himself listens; He himself is the true teacher.

He Himself is the tree
The flower and the fruit.
He Himself the bumble-bee
He Himself the land and water,
And He Himself the fish and the ocean.
His forms are indescribable.

He Himself the priceless jewel,
He Himself the connoisseur.
He Himself gives and takes away
He Himself punishes and forgives.
He Himself is the bow and the arrow.
He Himself the handsome archer.

He Himself is the speaker
Himself the listener.
He who has planned all things—
The air, the Guru. Water, the father.
Earth, the mother's womb.
Day and night, the nurses.
Love, the guardian.
Under these as he directs
The play of the world goes on.

He Himself the fish,
Himself the fisherman.
He Himself the cow,
He Himself the cowherd.
His light pervades all beings;
He directs all.

He Himself is the enjoyer
He Himself is the lover.
He Himself is the Yogi,
He Himself is the Lord of all,
Without form, without fear and suffering.
Himself the perfect Samadhi.

The whole creation is in Him,
All that is visible is subject to change.
He is changeless.
They indeed are true teachers
Who know the secret
And gather the wealth of His Name.

The secret of the Word
Is the gift of the True Teacher.
He is perfect with all powers.
He is in need of nothing.
He is eternal without trace of desire.
He is pure, and separate from all.

The true Guru, the giver of knowledge,
Whatever is seen is in Him.
Nanak begs at His door
For the gift of the Name.
They who have tasted the Nectar of the Name
Are intoxicated with it.
They are freed from birth and death.
To His devotees He gives peace and salvation.

True are Your regions and true Your universe.
True Your worlds and true Your creation.
True Your acts and all Your thoughts.
True Your order and true Your court.
True Your command and true Your behest.
True Your favors and true Your songs.
Hundreds of thousands and millions declare You true.
True is all Your power, true all Your strength,
True Your praises, true Your eulogies.
True Your might, O True King,
Nanak, true are they who meditate on the True One
That which is born and dies is not true.

They who knew the truth needed no more discussions and explanations. They gloried in the presence of a living teacher and enjoyed his company and then on the appointed day, they all departed.
Some to their homes in the perpetual snows, others to their monas-
teries and secluded dwelling places, while the Guru accompanied by
the Lama made his way through the high Himalayas, back to the
plains, to the world of men, to relieve the sorrow and suffering of
the world and to show the way of everlasting peace.

 YOGIS IN THE LAP OF THE GLACIERS

The Guru next traveled from Lake Mansarowar and Mt. Kailas
towards Almora and somewhere in the lap of the glaciers met a party
of Yogis—with their Guru, Gorakh Nath. They were said to possess
great power over nature and to know the secret of prolonging life,
retaining vigor of both body and mind.

They received the Guru with courtesy and invited him to stay
with them. "Why don't you join us?" said one of the Yogis. "We will
show you how to live through the ages and never grow old. We will
teach you to become a true Yogi."

"Can you show me nothing better than to prolong agony by

living a long time? I thought a Yogi sought freedom from bondage and was one with God. Know that Yoga is a spiritual union and can be achieved by abiding by His will and remaining unaffected by the impurities of the world. It is good to be in the world and not to be soiled by the evils of the world. You will admit," the Guru continued, "that the object of Yoga is union. This union cannot be accomplished by wandering in the forests or by physical austerities but by submerging the individualized ego in its divine source."

"You," said one of the Yogis, "profess to be a teacher of religion, yet you wear neither the clothes of a saint nor those of a Yogi. To what denomination do you belong?"

"My name is Nanak," said the Guru, "and I belong to the denomination of God."

"A householder must act for the self and thus make Karma, which must bring him back to earth to go through the cycle of birth and death. How can anyone without renouncing the world destroy the seed of action? Without its destruction, there is no freedom," said another Yogi.

"There is a great distinction between an assertive action and performance of an act without desire for its fruit," said the Guru. "The former binds, the latter frees. He whose mind is charged with the Divine Presence, he is in perpetual solitude in this world of desire. His thirst for things has been quenched. He who has realized the Unknowable and enabled others to realize Him, he commands respect. He is like a lotus that rises to the surface of a lake or like a swan that floats over the water and is untouched by water. So does a Yogi remain unaffected by his surroundings. He whose consciousness becomes one with the universal consciousness is, even when performing material acts, never moved from the stability which he has attained."

"Please do not be annoyed by our questionings," said the Yogi. We only seek to find the truth. We want to know if you have found a better way than ours."

"When this wandering mind is brought to the abode of Truth and His Name becomes its life-breath, then God Himself guides and shows the way of unity. He who is sinless, even though leading the life of a householder, whose spirit is awake, the thirst of whose mind is quenched with the nectar of the Name, the Guru shows him how to serve the True One and realize Him."

"How can anyone without proper preparation attain the unattainable?" asked another.

"I never said that," answered the Guru. "The seeker after Truth must prepare himself. He should not indulge in overeating or waste his day in sleep, but with a singleness of purpose concentrate on the True One, permeated with the sound of the true Word, freed from attachment and egoism, having banished passion, wrath, and pride, and with perfect self-control follow the Guru's instruction."

"You have said nothing about the ancient system of practicing Yoga," said another. "Don't you believe in its effectiveness?"

"I have heard of the system, but I do not believe that merely by outer restraints Yoga can be attained. What is needed is inner change. Let the soul draw itself into itself, close the nine doors, no longer run after sense objects, and take its seat in the tenth and hear the soundless sound, absorbed in the True One, see the True One in every heart, then the secret becomes manifest and reality is realized."

The Guru continued, "Evil thinking is destroyed only by dwelling on the Word of the Guru, who alone can show the gate to salvation. He who remains unaware of reality, continues to burn in the fire of desire. Separated by evil inclination, he suffers. Total submission to the Divine Will is more important than all the knowledge and virtues, and complete self-surrender is the way to secure Divine Grace."

"What do you mean by total submission?"

"Total submission is entire freedom from subjection to the three Gunas and becoming an instrument of the divine will with a heart full to the brim with God. Then the sense of I-AM-NESS vanishes and also the sense of separation."

"By what means does the mind remain stable. By what food is hunger satisfied forever?" asked another.

"He who is the same in pleasure and pain has attained stability of mind. He hungers no more. By God's grace death has no terror for him."

"How was the world created and how can its misery be removed?" asked another Yogi.

"The world exists in I-AM-NESS, in forgetting Him is the suffering. By the Guru's instructions control of mind is obtained, and sense of I-AM-NESS removed. Righteous aspirations gradually gather the treasures of Truth."

 ## FOOLS ARGUE ABOUT EATING MEAT

Thousands upon thousands of people had come to Kurukshetra to bathe in the sacred tank and pray that the sun might be saved from an eclipse. The Guru came in order to turn people from external ceremonies to inner purifications.

The Guru settled near the tank. A young prince who had been hunting in the neighborhood had killed a deer, and, as he passed the Guru, he offered him a piece of venison. The Guru accepted it and asked Bala to cook it. Bala was surprised but obeyed. A great crowd gathered round him. This was a sacrilege, which had never been committed before, and on a day when the Sun God was being harassed by his enemies. Nanak was besieged by angry Brahmins and others who were ready to stone him. The Guru stood up and spoke; the crowd stood spell-bound.

"I am doing this to show you that this matter is of no account. They who harbor in their hearts evil thoughts and under the cloak of abstinence aspire to holy living, know not the truth. They who wash the outside of the cup which is filled with pride, wrath and hate cannot become saints till they empty it of these. Hypocrites do not find the gateway to the True One.

> Fools wrangle about eating meat.
> They know not the truth, or the way of right action,
> Or the difference between meat and vegetables,
> And acts that are sinful and those that are sinless.
> They in ancient days killed rhinoceros
> And offered its flesh at the sacrificial fire.
> They, the man-eaters, pitiless and cruel,
> Hold their noses and forswear flesh.
> Is it any good telling the blind
> Who cannot see or act upon what is right?

"You call those who disagree with you blind," exclaimed a Brahmin with deep resentment.

"They are indeed blind," said the Guru, "who act blindly, whose hearts are unawakened. They who would see their parents starve and do nothing to relieve them but raise their voices in holy horror if anyone eats meat.

"Man is born of flesh, nursed in flesh, is a tabernacle of flesh. Men call themselves Pandits without knowledge and without doing what is right. The eating of meat is sinful, but the gratification of greed is held good. All living things are of flesh and have their being in flesh. They who follow a blind teacher eat eagerly what is unlawful and refrain from that which is lawful. Men and women seeing each other become slaves of lust."

The words of the Guru possessed the mind of the crowd and they felt what they had never felt before, that it was more important to banish cruelty from the mind than abstain from eating meat.

"You care for the shell and disregard the spirit;" continued the Guru, "for you untruth has become truth. Lead a righteous life and serve others. Such is the true path. If anyone salutes another, let him salute in the name of the Creator—Kartar—and respond in the same manner saying 'Sat Kartar'—'God is the only truth'."

They who came to stone the Guru became his disciples and established a Dharamsala, wherein God's Name could be recited and the weak and weary could find shelter.

In Kushwant Ghat, Guru Nanak saw a multitude of people offering water towards the East with their right hands. He moved forward, stood facing the priests and began to offer water towards the
West and with his left hand.

One of the priests moved forward and said, "You fool, what
are you doing? Come, I will help you to do what is right."

"I am doing just what you are doing," replied the Guru, and
continued offering water towards the West.

"We are offering water to the departed," said the priest, "to
quench their thirst."

"Then I am offering water to quench the thirst of my land,"
said the Guru.

The priest laughed and said, "How can water from here reach
your land in the Punjab?"

The Guru stopped, as a crowd had gathered around him. "If
the water I throw cannot reach my land, which is on this earth, how
can the water you throw reach ancestors who are no longer of this
earth and are no longer troubled by the hungers of the body?"

"How stupid you are," said the priest. "It is through the power
of chanting that the ancestors receive what is offered. We hold this
supreme secret. You cannot water your fields by splashing water
from here. Come, do something for your ancestors."

"You trade on the beliefs of men and women," said the Guru.
"You know that you know nothing. You have forsaken the right
path and claim to secure paradise for those that are gone, by throwing water toward the sun and other useless ceremonies. You have forgotten the Creator and his sacred Name. How can those who have
not saved themselves save others? You are preparing yourself for
hell."

This simple truth struck home. The crowd for a while stood
spell-bound and then an old priest strode forward. "How dare you
speak like this? It is you whom hell will claim. You who bear no
caste marks and look like neither a Hindu nor Muslim. We are Brahmins and worship gods and goddesses as ordained. We are custodians
of the divine secret. We follow what the holy books ordain."

The Guru sweetly smiled and said, "Anger is not the attribute
of those who follow holy scriptures. The custodians of Truth must
have control over their senses. They who perform ceremonies with
no love of God or man in their hearts and receive money in return
are doomed. Learn to worship God, to love His creation. The door
to paradise cannot be opened by splashing water but by selfless action and by absorption in the Sacred Word."

The crowd listened with rapt attention. The priests retreated, leaving the Guru. He sat surrounded by pilgrims, calmly teaching them the ways of Truth, when one asked, "What is superstition?"

"I will show you," said the Guru. He got up and approached a Brahmin who had drawn a circle round him and was cooking his food.

"May I come within your circle," asked the Guru, "and take some firewood?"

"Get away," he shouted. "If you step within my circle you will pollute my food."

"This is superstition," proclaimed the Guru. "This Brahmin has drawn a circle and considers that by so doing he is keeping out impurities. He is refusing to admit people of lower caste than himself, but he has all the pollution about him in spite of his circle. What can be more polluting than prejudice, cruelty, a slanderous heart and the fire of anger? And these are with him in spite of his circle."

"Teach us the right way," the crowd asked with folded hands.

"Listen," said the Guru full of joy. "Draw the circle of Truth, self-restraint and good acts around you, occupy the place of Truth and bathe in the pool of the Sacred Name."

"SAINTS ARE PURE WITHOUT BATHING"

Guru Nanak reached Allahabad and settled near Sangam, the junction of the rivers Ganges and Jumna where great crowds gathered to bathe. The Guru, however, made no attempt to bathe. A man who had been watching him was shocked at this behavior.

"Are you demented?" he asked. "Why don't you get up and bathe? This opportunity will never happen again."

"What opportunity?" asked the Guru.

"The opportunity of washing away your sins," said the man. The Guru answered:

> They are not pure who wash their bodies;
> They are indeed pure in whose hearts He dwells.
> They who come to bathe in holy water
> With minds full of deceit and hands ready to steal,
> Their outer dirt may be washed by bathing,
> But they increase the inner dirt twofold,
> Like a brass vessel that is polished without
> But is full of poison within.
> Saints are pure without bathing;
> Thieves remain thieves in spite of it.

Next to where the Guru sat, a Pandit, his body smeared with sandalwood paste, displayed his idols on a small altar. He sat with his eyes closed and only opened them when someone made an offering to the idols.

The Guru was greatly amused. "What do you see when you close your eyes?" he asked.

"In my Samadhi," replied the Pandit, "I see the three worlds. Please don't disturb my meditation." Thus saying he closed his eyes.

The Guru asked Bala to remove his altar. When he again opened his eyes he found his altar gone. He turned to the Guru and asked, "Tell me who has stolen my altar."

"Close your eyes and find it," replied the Guru.

"Please do not torment me," he pleaded almost in tears.

"I won't," said the Guru. "Your altar is safe, but is your soul? You are a learned man. Yet in spite of learning, you stoop to deceive others for the sake of a few pennies. My friend, collect the wealth of the Sacred Name. Save yourself and save others."

> He indeed is a fool
> Whose mind thirsts for money
> Who cries when money is lost.
> Only rare ones gather true wealth,
> The wealth of the Sacred Name,
> Inspired with true devotion.
> They are drenched in the color of the Sacred Name.
> They offer their mind and soul to God
> And take refuge in Him.

TO BENARES – THE ABODE OF SHIVA

Benares was said to be the abode of Shiva. It was believed that anyone who died on its sacred soil went straight to heaven. Also, it was a great seat of learning.

When Guru Nanak arrived in Benares, his garments, which were neither those of a householder nor of a monk, and his Hindu and Muslim companions attracted attention. A couple of learned Pandits came to him to hold discussions on various systems of philosophy.

"My dear Pandit," asked the Guru, "how does a sinner by merely dying here attain salvation?"

"He who touches the garment of Shiva becomes pure. A sinner no longer remains a sinner when he reaches Benares."

"You are learned in the six systems of philosophy," said the Guru. "Does anyone who reads or listens to the recital of Patanjali's Yoga become a Yogi and acquire powers?"

"No," said the Pandit, "only practice of Yoga endows a Yogi with power."

81

"Does it not follow that salvation cannot be attained by dwelling in a place but by working for it? Just as a Vedantist does not become Brahma by the mere assertion that he is a Brahma."

"Tell me then;" said the Pandit, "we read the Vedas and acquire knowledge. Why doesn't our knowledge blossom into flower and bear fruit?"

"You read and you recite but you rarely realize Truth. Mere lip service is of little avail. You never grasp even the real importance of the words you read. Then you perform endless ceremonies to secure enjoyment and greatness and feed the fire of desire, thus sowing fresh seeds of Karma, but you make no attempt to be one with Him, by serving His creation. Every selfish action forges fetters and binds the soul to the cycle of birth and death. The recitation of Mantras, the repetition of the Sacred Name impelled by whirlwinds of desire is of no use in the wilderness of the world. As long as passion, attachment, hate and pride preside, the reading of the scriptures and telling the rosary are of no avail. It is like clinging to a carcass which is without life.

> Worshipping a stone God,
> Displaying a rosary of sacred beads,
> Is like watering barren soil.
> Why waste life in empty formalities
> And plaster the body from without
> When it is crumbling from within?
> Fill the mind with charitable thoughts,
> Make a raft of the Sacred Name,
> Become bountiful and cross the ocean of life.
> Make your body like a Persian wheel,
> Harness your mind to its yoke,
> Draw the nectar and irrigate the soil of the mind.
> Change passion and anger into digging tools;
> With them rid the soil of the weeds.
> The deeper you dig, the greater will be the harvest.
> Thus learn the art of spiritual husbandry.
> Honest labor earns its reward.
> Even a heron by divine grace can become a swan.
> Thus prays Nanak, Your humble devotee,
> Bestow Your bounty, bountiful One!

The Pandit said, "You speak as if you know all, but have you read the Vedas and Shastras?"

"Listen to the truth," said the Guru.

A man may carry a cart-load of books,
He may have books all around him,
He may carry books in boat-loads,
Or fill empty caves with books.
He may read books for months and for years,
He may read them throughout his life,
Till breath leaves his body.
Nanak says only one Word is of account,
All else is for the glory of the self.

"Do you hold then that the study of Vedas and Shastras is of no use?"

"It is of no use unless what they teach is practiced. They are like beacon lights in surrounding darkness. Would it help a man who has lost his way to gaze at the light without taking the road which the light is destined to show?"

"How can one take the right road," asked the Pandit, "without proper exploration?"

When a true teacher is found,
Real peace is gained
And God's Name enters the heart.
Hope and fear depart.
The Sacred Word destroys I-AM-NESS.
By Divine Grace this gift is granted.

The crowd that had gathered treasured every word that the Guru uttered. They felt they understood that the ego was the center and source of attraction and repulsion, of suffering and pain, hope and fear. But the ego escaped these by submission to the Divine Will and gained freedom by absorption in His Name.

 ## RIDICULOUS CEREMONIES

From Benares the Guru slowly traveled to Gaya, which was associated with Lord Buddha. There a stronghold of Hindu priests declared that any offerings made at a particular place on the river secured absolution for those who had departed from the earth.

They professed to feed ancestors by offering rice-balls, lit little lamps to light their path in the heavens and performed other prolonged ceremonies.

The Guru stood on the banks of the river Sarju and watched them. Suddenly he burst into loud laughter.

The priests engaged in the solemn ceremonies were surprised.

"What are you laughing at?" they asked angrily.

Nanak answered, "Don't you see how ridiculous your ceremonies are? Those who have left this body, do they need food, do they need the glow of a lamp to see where neither the sun nor the moon shed their light? They see without sunlight just as you see without light when you dream."

"The essence of food reaches them and the lamps we light illuminate their darkness," asserted the priest. "Come, do your duty to your forefathers."

"I make no such offering and light no lamps," said the Guru.

> Brimful with the oil of suffering is the lamp of life.
> Kindle the flame of the Name.
> The flame of the Sacred Name
> Will consume the oil of sufferings,
> And the Lord Himself will be seen.
> For those whose hearts are steeped
> In the ocean of the Name,
> Bathing in Ganges and Jumna is of no use.
> He indeed is made clean by bathing
> Who adores Him night and day.
> The Brahmin makes rolls,
> Offers them to ancestors and to God,
> But eats them himself.
> Says Nanak, the roll of divine grace
> Is everywhere and forever satisfying.

The truth of what the Guru said touched the people's hearts, and the priests were frightened that they would desert them and follow the Guru.

"You are not wiser than the sages who gave us the scriptures. You are criticizing in the light of human understanding, but what the scriptures teach is beyond the bounds of human understanding," countered the priests.

"You follow the scriptures when it suits you," answered the Guru. "You follow what is convenient and profitable but you shun the call for sacrifice. Do your scriptures recommend indulgence in lust and greed? If you are learned in the scriptures, tell me, what is truth? Point out the difference between the path of darkness and the path of light. You are not only untrue to yourselves, but you mislead others. You prevent people from taking the right path by showing easy methods of salvation. All such acts are sinful. How can you help those who are gone, when your own actions are not free from sin?"

The Guru and his followers were passing through the forests of Assam and were unable to find any food. One day Mardana in despair exclaimed, "Guru, you are of God, the formless and neither hunger nor thirst affects you. I am a mere mortal man. I must have food."

There was a soap-nut tree nearby. The Guru turned around and pointed to it, "Go and eat its fruit, but remember you are not to bring any with you."

Mardana was aware that the bitter nuts were not edible. At the same time he was aware that the Guru never uttered a word that was not true, so he followed his teacher's instructions, picked up a nut and with some hesitation put it into his mouth. He found it sweet. Then he climbed the tree and ate the nuts till his appetite was satisfied. But he forgot the Guru's instructions and took some with him.

The next day he again felt hungry and started eating the soap-nuts. Mardana found them so bitter that he began vomitting and lost his voice.

The Guru laughed, "This happens when greed prevails. You would not share the nuts even with your friend Bala." The Guru then touched him and he recovered his voice immediately.

CLOTHES DO NOT MAKE A YOGI

A group of Sidha Yogis came to see the Guru in the hope of converting him. Their leader Bhartari came and sat near Nanak.

"Why do you wander like a Yogi," he said, "and yet refuse to enter our fold? Come I will put earrings on your ears, clothe you in the garments of a Yogi, make you a perfect Sidha, with occult powers and teach you how to live forever."

"What! Is it necessary to pierce my ears to make me a Yogi?" asked the Guru greatly amused. "I thought Yoga was the union of the individual spirit with the divine spirit, not a matter of a change of garments. My friends, outward forms and physical exercises are of no use as long as the ego rules. Make your mind free of egoism, pride, attachment and anger, before you begin teaching others."

Bhartari, the witness of ages, was annoyed to be questioned by young Nanak. "Listen, I inherit the wisdom of centuries, our system has endured from the beginning of time and its truth has never been challenged."

"I beg you not to be annoyed," said the Guru. "Age is no evidence of the intrinsic merit of any system. Have not good and evil existed side by side from the beginning of time? Your system does not eradicate the five evils: passion, anger, greed, attachment and desire."

"Have you any real power beyond words?" asked Bhartari.

"None," said the Guru. "I can do nothing against the law of God. It is only He who can perform a miracle."

"Bah," said Bhartari. "You see my disciple sitting in front of you, watch him. He will rise up to the skies, and become invisible in a moment. If you have any power, bring him back to earth."

The disciple in a moment flew upward, and was soon out of sight. Bhartari turned to the Guru, and said, "Find him."

"Hide and seek is a game for children. Wait and see." As Nanak said this, his two sandals flew up and in a short while the disciple descended, the sandals beating him down. Bhartari and his followers couldn't stop the beating. The disciple fell at the Guru's feet.

Then all of a sudden the Guru disappeared and Bhartari himself went in search of him. After a long time he returned. "I have searched the earth and the water and the high heavens," he said, "but I cannot find Guru Nanak." Just as he said this he found the Guru seated where he was before.

"Where did you hide yourself," inquired Bhartari full of astonishment.

"I was with you all the time," said the Guru. "The body dissolved itself into its elements and the soul into the all-soul."

The Sidhas were overwhelmed with awe and sat spell-bound.

KAUDA, THE MAN-EATING BHEEL

On purpose the Guru lost his way and ended up in a thick forest which was inhabited by a tribe of Bheels who ate human flesh. His two companions were tired, hungry and depressed, and at their request the Guru sat under a tree. Mardana, as usual, was famished and after a little rest started to look for something to eat.

"There are wild men living in this forest, so be careful where you go," the Guru warned him.

"You are Nanak Nirankari, God's own," said Mardana. "You are not affected by hunger and pain, I am a mere man and subject to both."

"Mardana had gone a distance when Kauda, a notorious cannibal, met him. Kauda kept oil boiling in a big pan to roast his victims. He saw Mardana from a distance and was delighted at the prospect of a good meal. Kauda took Mardana by surprise and in an instant tied him up with the rope he carried. He then carried him to the spot where his pan was boiling.

Mardana prayed to the Guru to save him. The Guru already

knew of his distress and was on his way to him. He arrived just as Kauda was preparing to throw Mardana into the boiling oil.

Kauda stopped when he saw Nanak and Bala approaching. He thought he had two more victims and he rushed towards them swinging his rope. As he approached, the Guru raised his hand and Kauda stopped dead, trembling from head to foot. He fell on the ground unable to move looking up helplessly with his large wild eyes, entirely bewildered. Bala meanwhile released Mardana.

Then the Guru turned to Kauda and commanded him to rise. Kauda slowly raised himself and then fell at the feet of the Guru and prayed for mercy. He said, "It has been foretold that a man of God would save my soul."

"God is all-merciful," said the Guru. "He is all compassionate. He forgives all those who repent and abstain from doing wrong."

"I will do as you bid me," said Kauda. "Accept me as your disciple."

"Listen," said the Guru, "and act on what I tell you and thus win grace. Learn that attachment, greed, anger and harmfulness are the four streams of fire. These consume mankind. Only virtuous action can quench the fire and open the treasures of bliss.

"From now on resolve to harm no one, be merciful and serve all those who need your service. Concentrate your mind on the Creator, learn to love Him with all your heart and mind, just as lovers do, and make His Name the sustenance of your life."

Kauda was completely converted and to the end of his days was a devout disciple of the Guru.

 ## THE QUEEN OF THE BLACK MAGICIANS

Kamroop was ruled by a queen who, along with all her subjects, practiced black magic and exercised supernatural powers. The Guru and Bala made themselves comfortable under a tree while Mardana went into town to get some food. He had not gone far when he encountered a party of three gaily dressed women, who asked, "How and why have you come to our town?"

Mardana answered in his rustic Punjabi, which they could not understand. His manner and dress amused them. "He bleats like a lamb," said one of the women.

Another laughed and said, "I will make him a lamb," and saying this she took out a thread, breathed something on it and threw it over Mardana's neck and commanded, "Now become a lamb and bleat."

Mardana instantly stood on all fours and began to bleat. All three women clapped their hands and burst into laughter.

The Guru had seen what had happened to his companion and when the women saw him and Bala coming, they were greatly amused. "We shall turn all of them into animals," they said. "I will make that young man bark like a dog."

She approached Bala and was about to put the thread round his neck when the Guru said, "Become that on which your thoughts are fixed."

The woman at once went on all fours and began to bark like a dog.

The Guru told Bala to remove the thread from Mardana's neck, then utter Sat Nam and sprinkle some water on him. Immediately Mardana stood up and wiped the beads of perspiration from his face.

The second woman attempted to throw a rope round Bala's neck but as she lifted her arm, it remained fixed in position. The third woman moved to her assistance but found that the jar she was carrying over her head was fixed as if by cement.

A fourth woman saw what had happened and ran to the Queen to report that a great magician had arrived and rendered their powers useless.

The Queen herself came to the spot and in all sorts of ways tried to work her magic, but to no avail. She couldn't cast a spell on the Guru or his companions, nor could she release the three women. A great crowd gathered around them and all were terrified by the Guru's power.

The Queen then bowed before the Guru, placed a pile of gold and jewels in front of him and prayed, "Great magician, accept me as your disciple, teach me your magic, and release my sisters."

The Guru told her to take away her gold. The Queen then fell at his feet and prayed for mercy.

"You ask for mercy and it will be shown to you. You must promise to abandon your wicked practices of black magic and seek refuge in God." So saying the Guru uttered Sat Nam, sprinkled a little water on the three women, and they were restored to their normal condition.

"See, your goddess has given you the power of doing mischief without any power of healing suffering hearts."

"You are great," said the Queen. "What you say is true."

"God alone is great," said the Guru, "He creates, maintains and withdraws this universe unto Himself. We suffer when we follow the wrong way and do evil. When we turn to Him and follow the golden rules of life, we become virtuous and earn our reward in happiness."

"Great one, we have been misled. We have followed the traditions of our tribe."

"That is why I have come—to lead you to the right way," said the Guru.

The Guru then told them to purify their bodies and minds by dethroning hate, covetousness and jealousy from the mind and replacing them with sympathy and love. "Become queens of mercy," he said. "Man is always going astray. You can make a paradise for him on earth and help his ascent by your own example, by holy living and the magic of self-surrender. You can open for him the gates of Heaven by your own devotion. You can teach him the meaning of love by your own selflessness. You are goddesses in your own right. Worship no ugly images, but fulfill your divine mission to sow in the hearts of boys and girls the seed of virtue and teach them by your own way of living that courage and truth are rooted in their being. No syllable of religion is ever understood but through a virtuous deed."

 ## "LEARN TO LOVE ONE ANOTHER"

In Jagannath, towards evening, he entered the temple and sat in a corner of the inner court. As soon as the sun set, priests and pilgrims gathered in great numbers and performed the evening ceremonial service by burning incense, blowing conches, ringing bells and waving lights. The Guru took no part in the ceremony; he never even moved.

"Are you ill?" inquired a priest approaching him when the ceremony was over. "Why didn't you join in the offering to the Lord?"

"Where is the Lord?" asked the Guru.

"Are you blind? The statue of the Lord is before your very eyes?"

"Am I blind? Tell me how can a statue of wood represent the Lord of the universe? He who is beyond human imagination. He is boundless—all-pervading."

"Beware of what you say," shouted several voices.

"I speak the truth," exclaimed the Guru. "The lord of the universe does not dwell in wooden statues, crudely put together by carpenters. The Lord of the universe dwells in every heart. He pervades all that is and the whole universe worships Him. He is the Unknowable, the All-merciful, the Creator. I worship and perform his ceremony.

"The Lord of the universe is not confined in one place, house or temple. The sky, the earth, no, the whole universe with all its planets and millions of stars, earths, suns and moons are His. He is all-pervading. He creates and He, in destroying, recreates. There is no end to His greatness. The whole universe bows before Him. It is His light that is in the sun and the moon. It is His light which is in each of us. Seek it within your hearts. It is manifested in the Shabad—the Name. Therefore take refuge in the Sacred Name, charge every breath with His Name till self is submerged in its sound and through His grace salvation is attained."

The Guru walked out of the temple followed by the pilgrims. Mardana asked for some water to drink. The Guru stopped where he stood and said, "Dig where you stand and you will discover a spring of sweet water."

Mardana obeyed and the other people joined him and after some digging, a spout of sweet water flowed forth near the sea and the whole crowd drank from it.

The Guru stayed for three days and taught the people. When on the third day he was about to depart, the people asked him to give a parting message.

"Act in the light of Buddhi—the higher wisdom—and follow the path of righteousness, control the five senses and restrain them from the pursuit of sense-objects. Keep a vigilant watch on the mind, lest the fire of desire consume the self. Above all, take refuge in Him and invoke His Name. He is pleased when in others we see the face of a brother and extend the help which we wish others to extend to us. The more this feeling of fellowship grows, the nearer we draw to God. There is no other way but this, that we learn to love one another and thus find the secret of loving God."

THE ENEMY OF ANCIENT DHARMA

The Guru traveled farther south and at last reached the sea, stopping at Rameshwar. There were sadhus in groups, some with their families, occupying various resting places along the beach.

They were greatly intrigued by the unorthodox appearance of the Guru and his two companions. They could not figure out their religion. The leader of one of these groups, unable to suppress his curiosity, approached the Guru and asked, "To which denomina- do you belong? What is your name?"

"My name is Nanak Nirankari, and I belong to the denomination tion of the Formless," he answered.

The leader was struck by the youthfulness and saintly expression of the Guru's face and decided to convert him.

"My good boy," he said in coaxing tones, "there is something in you that attracts me. Come and be my disciple and some day I will make you the greatest of renunciates. I will place the idol Thakurjee in your keeping."

The Guru smiled and said, "How can you place the Lord of all creation in my keeping? He in whose keeping is the whole universe."

"But Thakurjee is the symbol of the Lord. In worshipping him in stone, we recognize his presence in all things," said the leader.

"He is in all things," said the Guru, "but all things found manifestation through the Word and it is through the Sacred Word alone that we can reach Him."

A great crowd of women and children gathered around the Guru.

"Dear friends," said the Guru, "recite the Sacred Name, seek the true guru and see the Lord with your own eyes."

"You lay down the law," said the leader, "as if you saw the past, present and future. Tell me what holds the whole creation?"

"The tentacles of attachment enmesh all creation. Salvation is attained by freeing the self from attachment. Father and mother, son, daughter, wife and their children are chains that bind mankind. The farmer who produces and contributes to the revenue of the State, the trader who works for profit, and the banker who hoards money are all bound by attachment. All actions, all duty performed in the interest of self, all reading of holy scriptures to aggrandize the self become the cause of bondage. These increase the sense of self-hood. There is no escape from bondage," says Nanak, "without taking shelter in the Sacred Name, devotion to God and protection of the Guru."

"Maya," continued the Guru, "deludes the self in infinite varieties of ways, by attachment to relatives, desire to accumulate wealth, and ambition to become powerful and great. The soul of man thus forges chains which hold him to earth. It is only when the illusions of Maya fade and obsess the mind no more, that Truth is realized and the soul of man finds refuge in God."

"How can a man seek salvation without performing good actions such as the worship of idols and the performance of ceremonies as laid down in holy books?" asked a Pandit who had come to listen to the conversation. "By abandoning these we seal our own doom."

"You are learned in the ancient lore," replied the Guru. "Look within your own heart and admit that these acts are inspired by desire and forge the chains of Karma which hold the soul to the cycle of birth and death."

"You seem to have no regard for the teaching of Vedas and Shastras," spoke the Pandit with anger. "It's not right to listen to your seductive speeches."

"I speak the truth," said the Guru. "What is the good of your talking about the teachings of Vedas, when you ignore their teachings and perform acts that bind the soul? The dirt of sensuous acts is not removed by mere performance of ceremonial acts. You weave like spiders the web that entangles others and destroys them and

"I cannot listen to you any more," said the Pandit rising. "You are a trouble-maker. Men like you are enemies of ancient Dharma and should be avoided."

The crowd that had gathered round the Guru beseeched him to tell them more.

"There is nothing more to tell," said the Guru. "One word of Truth is enough if you treasure it in your hearts. It has the power to convert the soul from selfishness to selflessness."

> If we churn milk
> We produce its essence—butter.
> If we churn water we produce nothing.
> This is the substance of truth.
> Without the Guru, doubt is not dispelled,
> And the Infinite dwelling in every heart is not discovered.
> The world is like a cotton thread,
> Enmeshing all things within its net.
> The Guru alone can untie its knots.
> All other acts are of no use.
> This universe is cheated by desire.
> What else can one say?
> When the Guru is found,
> Fear of God enters the mind,
> The reality of death is realized.

DANCING GIRLS IN CEYLON

On the island kingdom of Ceylon off the shore of Rameshwar lived Rajah Shive Nabh, who was anxious to become a disciple. His friend Bhagirath, a trader from India, and a disciple of the Guru, had told him about Guru Nanak and his wonderful power of leading people on to the true path. The Rajah asked Bhagirath how he could meet the Guru.

He replied, "If you concentrate your mind and with purity of heart pray for his presence, he will not fail to fulfill your desire."

Every morning Shive Nabh prayed earnestly for the Guru to reveal himself to him in person. He was told that the Guru enjoyed staying out under open skies, so he planted a grove of shady trees for his comfort. Many persons who claimed to be gurus came and stayed in the grove but were found to be charlatans. Days ran into months, months into years, but there was no trace of the Guru. Shive Nabh almost lost hope and neglected the grove so that some of its trees began to shed their leaves and wither.

One day, feeling the Rajah's longing, the Guru with a group of disciples stood on the seashore at Rameshwar and said, "A friend of mine is waiting to meet me on the other side. I must go across and reward his long devotion."

"How can we do so?" asked the disciples.

"If the Sacred Name has the power to enable all men to cross the ocean of death, that Name can take you across this small span of water. Utter Wahe Guru, repeat Ek Ong Kar, the true Word, the creative spirit, free of fear and hate, timeless, birthless, self-existent." So saying, the Guru walked over the surface of the water and asked the others to follow him. Bala and Mardana obeyed. The waves were hushed and opened a path for the Guru. They moved swiftly as if the air itself were carrying them to the other side.

In due time they touched land and the Guru walked to the grove which Shive Nabh had dedicated to him. As soon as he entered the grove the withered trees sprouted green foliage.

The news reached Shive Nabh that a holy man had arrived. He had been deeply disappointed by men who wore spiritual dress but were deceptive and unredeemed within. He now followed a well-conceived plan of testing whether the guest was really the Guru or some impostor. He ordered two of his most beautiful dancing-girls to visit the Guru and tempt him with their charms. Only if they failed to seduce him would he then visit the holy man himself.

The girls approached the grove dressed in colorful garments. They were full of laughter and mischief, carrying baskets of flowers to offer the Guru, sure of conquest, proud of their beauty and the magic of their passionate music to enchant him, as they had done in the case of many a wandering ascetic. As they entered the grove, an indescribable calmness possessed their minds and robbed them of their seductive purpose. They walked humbly to the place where the Guru sat, bowed to him in all humility and sat respectfully at a distance from him. The sweet music which Mardana was playing, accompanied by the Guru's singing, entered their hearts. They sat spell-bound, like statues, as the Guru sang:

> O my mind, love the Lord
> As the lotus loves the water.
> The waves dash against it
> But its love is ever increasing.
> O my mind, how can you find release
> Without love to open the inner door,
> To receive the treasures of devotion?
>
> O my mind, love the Lord
> As the fish loves water,
> The deeper it dives, the happier it is.
> Its body and mind are at peace.

It cannot live a moment without water.
So must you live in the Lord—
He is aware of your travail.

O my mind, love the Lord
As the tree longs for the rain.
Though lakes may be overflowing
And the land green with foliage
Its thirst is not quenched
Without a rain-drop from the sky.
True love only grows on the soil of good action.

O my mind, love the Lord
As water loves milk.
Place it on the fire, it burns itself
But protects the milk.
He unites the separated selves,
He exalts the true one by His own grace.

O my mind, love the Lord
As the nightengale loves the moon
And the whole night
Calls for her mate from afar, who is near.
Minds possessed by self are never conscious of Him.
They whom the Lord enlightens are always in His presence.

The news reached the Rajah that the dancing-girls had passed under the Guru's spell. The Rajah hurried to the grove where he found the gates closed against him. He humbly prayed to be forgiven for his trespasses and to be admitted. The prayer was heard and the gate opened by itself. The Rajah entered and fell at the feet of the Guru.

"Teach me," he said. "I have waited for you for countless years."

The Guru asked him to rise. "I have come in response to your steadfast devotion," he said. "I knew you were waiting for me."

"I have long waited," repeated Shive Nabh. "Now you have come and all my longings are fulfilled."

"Driven by desire," said the Guru, "men calculate their gains. They do not realize that things happen as He ordains. The whole world values the transitory, and does not realize the value of reality. When true teaching reveals reality, only then is the truth discovered and the treasure of peace gathered."

"How is it," asked Shive Nabh, "that men wander without true devotion and fail to follow the right path?"

"Only the pure in heart can follow the path of devotion," said the Guru. "It is an act of complete self-surrender to the Lord, its reward is the wealth of knowledge of all that is in the three worlds. He who is a seeker of virtue never forgets the true Name."

"This world has an appearance of permanency," observed Shive Nabh, "and yet all that exists is in a state of flux."

"Even those fluttering birds who feed on pearls of knowledge from unfathomed depths have to depart. Everyone has to depart and may be called at any moment to leave this playground. He whom the Lord saves by His grace meets the true teacher and retires victoriously."

"How is it that the fire of devotion is not kindled in every heart," asked Shive Nabh.

"Without the true teacher," said the Guru, "the dirt of desire is not destroyed and devotion does not possess the mind. Devotion unlocks the secret of the Word. Soham—you are He—is revealed and with it knowledge of the self. A righteous man acquires knowledge of of the self. Nothing else is of any account."

"Do the devotees find union with the Lord?" asked Shive Nabh.

"Yes," said the Guru, "through the power of the Word they are in Him and need no uniting. The ignorant know not this truth and as separated selves suffer again and again. There is only one gate and one house. There is no other place."

 RAJA YOGA

During the Guru's stay on Ceylon people profited by his teachings. The Guru had noticed that the Rajah, the Rani, and a few others were anxious to hear about the practices of the Raja Yoga. He held that a seeker of Yoga should begin by securing seclusion where he could meditate without interruption. He should subdue the five senses, eat little, sleep moderately, dwell constantly on truth and by restraints of the body and mind awaken higher centers of consciousness.

"He who has brought the five senses under control," he said, "who never speaks untruth, who has brought the five passions, seven impediments, and nine gates under subjection is on the path of attainment. Out of millions who strive, only a rare one acquires the knowledge of the true One. The Yogi leads his consciousness to the innermost recesses of heart, and from there to the hidden brain-centers, where the three streams meet between the eyebrows. He draws the power that pulsates through the nerves known as Ida and Pingala, from the right to the left and unites them so that they become one. It is thus that his vision broadens and he sees the goal far away, and beyond it the supreme point which is difficult to attain.

His consciousness then perceives the nine spheres and all that exists in the four quarters—east, west, north and south."

"It is all so difficult," said the Rajah. "Tell me some simpler way."

"Make this body the container," said the Guru. "Pour into it the milk of human kindness. Leaven it with true aspiration and convert it into curds. Make discrimination the churn and the Sacred Name the churning rope and churn again and again and collect the butter. This is they way of Yoga."

"Please, tell me more about it," said the Rajah.

"A Yogi must rid himself of the darkness of desire and greed and allow the five passions to burn themselves out. He should keep the bow of true resolve constantly strung to destroy the self and its evil thoughts. He who repeats no other Mantra but God's Name, in him righteous tendencies grow strong and evil tendencies die of attenuation. He is never caught in the noose of death. Such is the characteristic of a true Yogi.

"He finds the right way to practice the Sacred Name and, when practiced with skill, it bestows perfection. Without skill it is unproductive like barren soil. Conquer the mind and with the dagger of knowledge destroy the five passions and place the wandering mind under restraint. He who learns the art of subduing the mind becomes a Renunciate."

"How can we know a Yogi?" asked the Rajah.

"He who is restrained, to whom gain and loss are the same, who neither rejoices nor sorrows, who does not waste his powers by clinging to earth, but keeps the kite flying upward till in the innermost recess of the brain the spirit buzzes like a bee. This is the characteristic of a Yogi.

"He is a Yogi who speaks of nothing else but of true knowledge and of God, and whose awakened consciousness is absorbed in meditation, throwing strings of devotion into the fathomless, to form a link with the Absolute. His lips no more express the sorrow of separation. Adoring the Lord, he by the grace of God becomes one with Him. Even lesser gods bow in obeisance to him. Such are the characteristics of a true Yogi."

"LEARN TO LIVE IN FEAR OF HIM"

Accompanied by Bala and Mardana, the Guru proceeded to Kanya Kumari at the tip of India. On arriving there, he sat on a hill near the temple of the goddess. He had not been there long when he saw a large crowd hurrying with offerings to the goddess. The priests had let it be known that she was angry, so people from all the neighboring villages were coming to try and regain her favor. Some of them came up to the Guru and begged him to accompany them and intercede on their behalf.

The Guru laughed and said, "You foolish people, why are you afraid of gods and goddesses and not afraid of Him who has created the universe. You think you can please the stone statue by your offerings, which are of no use to the idol. Learn to be afraid of Him who sees all your thoughts and actions and metes out justice. In His court men are judged by their actions, the righteous find favor and are freed and the unrighteous reap the harvest of their own sowing. Learn to live in fear of Him."

> In fear fire performs its forced labor,
> In fear winds and breezes blow.
> In fear flow hundred thousands of rivers,
> In fear the earth bears its burdens,
> In fear Indra moves unceasingly.
> In fear is the sun, in fear is the moon.
> They travel millions of miles without end.
> In fear are the Sidhas, the Buddhas, the demi-gods
> In fear are the stars and the firmament,
> Warriors and mighty men and divine heroes.
> In fear, streams of men
> Flow from the unmanifest to the manifest.
> God hath destined fear for everyone.
> Nanak, the formless, the True One alone is beyond fear.

The people stood spell-bound. The power of his words went to their hearts. The crowd grew and begged the Guru to teach them. Speaking in the language of the people he said: "Do not let your spiritual emotion be wasted worshipping stone gods and goddesses. Worship Him, the Lord of all creation. He is not to be won by offerings. He demands complete purification and dedication of body and mind. You worship Him when you are aware that He is in all things. When you see Him in all beings you begin to love His creation and love one another. Then all quarrels, wars and cruelties come to an end. Earth is His kingdom. Joy and true happiness are His gifts. He is within you. Make your hearts pure, repeat His Name and lose yourself in adoring Him."

The audience asked him to go on.

> He is indescribable, boundless, immeasurable.
> He is not subject to time or death.
> He is neither high caste nor low caste.
> He is unborn, self-existent .

He has no attachment or aversion.
I am a sacrifice to that True One
Whose actions are also true.
He has no form, color or mark.
The true Word is his only symbol.
He has no mother or father, nor wife, nor relations,
He is free from all desire.
He is beyond intellect, beyond all Maya,
Beyond all and everything.
His light is in all directions.
In every being is Brahma hidden,
In every heart is His light.
Under the instruction of the teacher,
Closed gates are flung open,
And undistrubed Samadhi is attained.
All creation exists in time,
Takes birth and dies,
As ordained by Him.
By the grace of Guru,
The key of the true teacher is given.
By the magic of the Word, liberation is obtained.

"It is only when your vessel becomes pure that it is filled by the True One. There is one in a million who knows the mystery of self-surrender, and thus becomes one with the Supreme, and then the human soul becomes one with Supreme soul."

Those who listened became converted by the truth of the Guru's teachings and became his disciples. They discarded the worship of all gods and goddesses except the one supreme Being.

THE RANI

Next the Guru came to a province ruled by a Rani who was learned in the lore of the Hindu religion. She was not only learned but charitable and had built a dharamsala where strangers and holy men were welcomed and entertained.

As was his practice, the Guru stayed in a grove outside the town. The news reached the Rani that a holy man had arrived and she sent a messenger to invite the Guru to the dharamsala. He thanked the Rani for her invitation but said he was happy where he was.

The Rani considered it a privilege and her duty as a ruler to meet holy men and to entertain them so she came out to see Nanak. She bowed respectfully and said, "Good Sir, why have you refused my hospitality? Am I unworthy to serve you? Is my food unrighteously earned?"

"No," said the Guru. "You are worthy in every way. You gather your revenue and return it like rain for the benefit of your subjects. He who earns and gives away knows something of the Way. He who does not appropriate everything to himself but gives and induces others to give in the Name of God is blessed. He who shares his bread with others knows the law of living."

"Isn't it all an illusion? What is Maya? Is it real or unreal, sat or asat?" asked the Rani. She was well-versed in ancient literature.

"Ah! my daughter," said the Guru, "is your mind entangled in the web of these speculations? Only he who sees both the real and unreal can speak with authority."

> All His regions and His heavens are real.
> God's world and all His creation is real.
> All His thoughts and acts are real.
> All His laws and His judgments are real.
> All His commands and decrees are real.
> All His graces and symbols are real.
> Real is His power, real is His might,
> All that is manifest and is seen is real.
> Millions upon millions declare Him to be real.
> All His praises and powers are real.
> Nanak says they alone know reality
> Who meditate on the True One.

"If I have understood your meaning," said the Rani, "you hold that the Lord, the Creator, is real and, therefore, His manifestation cannot be unreal."

"Dear Rani," said the Guru, "it profits little to dwell on these theories. Know that He is real. Pursue the path of righteousness and get established in reality. They who are fascinated by the ever-changing and dwell on the ever-changing remain subject to brith and death."

"The learned," said the Rani, "the great Pandits, expound theories which are difficult to follow, but what you say seems true."

The Guru said, "There is only one thing to remember—learn to mold the mind so that it becomes fit to receive the divine light."

> They who clothe themselves in pure white
> With minds dark with evil thoughts
> And claim equality with those
> Who stand serving at the door,
> They make fair show in speech,

But indulge in evil action.
They who are absorbed in the Lord,
Imbued in His bliss, having attained power,
Are humble and meek.
Make your life worthy by joining such devotees.

"Discussions about realities are beyond the region of human intelligence and mere discourses on religion are of no avail unless virtuous actions purify the mind and make it fit for the realization of Truth. When darkness of the mind is thus removed, it is only then that the light of spirit can illumine it and in that light is seen the difference between the real and the unreal. By becoming one with the real, salvation is obtained."

The Rani bowed, perfectly satisfied. She ordered food which was brought by her servants. The Guru had the food distributed among the poor who had assembled outside the garden. The Rani was deeply concerned as the Guru distributed the food, for he was keeping nothing for himself.

The Guru read what was in the mind of his hostess. He turned to her and said, "My daughter, I am offering food to the Lord by appeasing the fire of hunger of his children."

ELEPHANT – RISE!

When passing through Delhi, Guru Nanak stopped for the night near an elephant stable. He heard loud wailing throughout the night. Early in the morning an elephant driver came to him and fell at his feet.

"Holy one," he wept, "I am ruined; my elephant died suddenly last night. I loved the animal. My children loved him and now I will lose my job and my children will starve."

The Guru was touched by the grief of the elephant driver and his love for the animal. "Go," he said, "say Sat Nam, touch the forehead of the elephant with your hand, and say 'Rise'."

The elephant driver obeyed and, to his surprise, when he said Sat Nam and put his hand on the elephant's forehead, the huge animal shivered and came to life.

The elephant driver and his family were filled with joy, and the news that the dead animal had been restored to life swiftly spread throughout the city. The news reached the King, Sikander Lodhi, who refused to believe it and came to see for himself. He was surprised when the elephant raised his trunk and saluted him. It was his favorite elephant. He was led by the elephant driver to the Guru. "Holy one, how did you breathe life into the dead animal?"

"I am of no account. It is only He who takes away life and restores it again."

"Can He take away life now?" asked the King incredulously.

"Perhaps, if you pray to the Almighty, he may listen to your prayers," the Guru said.

The King prayed and the elephant sank back and died.

"Great one, restore the elephant to life again," asked the King.

"Foolish King," said the Guru, "it is only He who can reanimate the dead. There is no other but God. His will be done. You were His instrument in praying for the death of the animal. Iron when heated in the fire becomes red and the hand cannot hold it for a moment. Men of God become red with compassion in the heat of His love and cannot be compelled into that mood again."

The King bowed his head and placed large offerings of money before the Guru.

"These are of no use to me," said the Guru. "I hunger for God, my wealth of love has no attraction for you and what you have has no attraction for me. God has quenched all my hungers while the fire within you grows the more it is fed by worldly possessions."

"Bless me, Great one," beseeched the King.

"He is blessed who makes his heart a temple for divine grace to enter. Sow no more the seed of cruelty. For what we sow we reap. Become a shadow of God on earth and serve His creation in faithfulness and truth. God's blessings will descend upon you."

In the meantime the Guru had been surrounded by Qazis and Pandits, who asked him to discuss religious and philosophic problems.

"How can I discuss truth amidst pervading hypocrisy and with men whose intellect is clouded by pride and falsehood?"

> They who profess to be religious
> Indulge in sinful acts.
> They who profess to teach
> Hasten to the homes of disciples,
> Instead of the disciple
> Seeking the teacher.
> Even the love of husband and wife
> Depends on what the husband can give.
> No one believes in holy scriptures,
> Everyone worships his own self.
> Such is this dark age.

From Delhi the Guru proceeded to Mathra, the birthplace of Lord Krishna. The Guru was in ecstasy as he entered the city. He walked to the river Jumna and the sight that met him grieved him greatly. The lanes and the banks of the river were crowded with beggars who had abandoned their Dharma and now lived on alms. A blind man was mixing a handful of ashes in an earthen bowl to drink. He was so emaciated that it was clear that he had gone without food for days. The Guru's heart was touched. "Why are you drinking ashes?" he asked.

"I have been down with fever," the man answered, "and haven't been able to go around and beg. I am starving. Have pity upon me."

"Yes," said the Guru. He took a handful of water, uttered the Name of God and sprinkled it on the blind man's eyes.

Instantly the blind man could see. He saw the Guru standing in front of him. He could not believe it.

"My dream has come true," he said. "I dreamed some days ago that a great teacher, Guru Nanak, would come and give me sight. You are Nanak, God's messenger." He continued through tears of gratitude, "I have done without eyes all my life and could have done so to the end, which couldn't be far off. Now give me the sight to find the way to God."

The Guru smiled and said, "You shall have it."

Soon the Guru was surrounded by a group of devotees, who were singing devotional songs and dancing, jumping, and going round in a circle. The Guru stopped and inquired, "What are they doing?"

"They are performing Kirtan," came the answer, "and are intoxicated with the love of God."

"The true devotees lose themselves in adoration of God and in a state of ecstasy may dance out of pure joy. They in whose heart the spark of devotion is covered with the dust of desire, merely jump about without the true impulse which moves the devotees of God. These men are merely play-acting without any overpowering joy of spirit."

The Guru turned to them and said, "The disciples play, the gurus dance, shake their feet and roll their heads; the dust that they raise falls on their heads. The dancers dash themselves on the ground and others clap their hands and keep time, all this for the sake of earning food. The audience watches their antics and laughs. Tell me, what spiritual and moral purpose do they serve?"

"Is there no meaning in the performance of these practices?" asked a villager.

"None," said the Guru. "Do oil presses, spinning wheels, hand-mills, potter's wheels, tops, churning staves, threshing frames, birds whirling in the air and whirlwinds have any spiritual significance? So men have no significance who turn round and round without the love of God. In life itself, innumerable men in unending streams turn the wheel of birth and death, bound by the chain of their acts. They dance their way to death. They who waste their days in laughter and dance will regret it, and weep when they depart. Nanak says that those who have fear of God in their minds also conceive the love of God in their hearts."

The Guru walked on and came to a spot where the drama of Krishna and his Gopis was being staged. He stopped and watched the play. It symbolized Lord Krishna and his devotees in the form of a boy lover and the maids who loved him. The play had meaning and spiritual value. The acting was good.

The Guru strode forward and said, "See how Krishna's love reaches all his devotees. He, the fearless, formless Lord, is one, while his devotees are numberless."

> Beat the drum
> With the hand of truth and contentment,
> Tie bells of everlasting joy to your feet.
> In the sound of soundless sound,
> Lose all sense of separation.
> Imbued with this, dance step by step.
> Any other dance is a physical peformance,
> Only he dances, who dances in perfect harmony of spirit.

> A mind filled with the fear of the Lord,
> Sitting and standing, remembers Him,
> Knowing that this body will turn to dust
> Imbued in this thought, step by step,
> Only he dances, who dances in perfect harmony of spirit.

> Treasure the true instruction
> Given in the company of the good,
> And the Sacred Name given by the Guru,
> Nanak says again and again,
> Imbued in this, dance step by step,
> Only he dances who dances in perfect harmony of spirit.

The Guru later sang:

> He indeed is a Brahmin
> Who sees Brahma in all,
> Who is restrained and devoted to Brahma,
> Who is established in calm content
> Who has broken the bonds and attained liberation.

Such a Brahmin is worthy of worship.
Actions determine caste;
Man exalts or lowers himself by his own acts.
By devotion to the Sacred Name
Release from the wheel of birth and death is obtained.
Do not worry about distinction of caste
Realize that His light is in all,
There is no caste on the other side.

Next morning Nanak sat on the river bank and a large crowd gathered round, eager to hear him.

"See the deep flowing stream, its big, tossing waves breaking into drops and yet they are one with the stream," said the Guru. "He who knows this also knows His creation is in Him and his own self shares the essence of divine life. He who knows this is on the way to salvation. In the darkness of the night is hidden the light of the day. This mystery is not resolved without the guidance of the Guru.

"Man is in woman and woman in man. Sound dwells in the silence and meditation itself is in sound. This mystery cannot be unravelled. Those who unravel it are beyond the power of description. The light is in the mind, the mind partakes of light. O brothers, this is discovered by the grace of the Guru. They indeed are blessed whose consciousness is submerged in the Sacred Name.

"The world is the shadow of self. Destroy the self, and with it will disappear the shadow which obscures the light and then perchance you will perceive the 'how and wherefore' of that which is beyond comprehension. The mind suffers from the obsession of selfhood, which burns with the fire of desire. When the mind is drawn back into the true self, the desire dies and with it all suffering ceases."

"MAKE THE SACRED NAME YOUR SUSTENANCE"

At Nasik, where the Guru stopped by the Godavri River, a banker approached him and offered him lodgings in his dharamsala which he had built for the comfort of pilgrims.

The Guru smiled and said, "The earth is my dharamsala, its canopy the sky and I am waiting for my host."

The banker was still there when a poor goldsmith approached the Guru and humbly asked, "Kind sir, will you bless my humble home with your presence? I can offer you nothing by way of comfort except my own humble service and my devotion."

The Guru turned to the banker. "See my host has arrived! I was waiting for him." So saying he rose and followed the goldsmith to his house.

It was a two-roomed hut with no furniture. One room was placed at the disposal of the Guru. The wife of the goldsmith brought water in an earthen jug; the goldsmith with great devotion washed the feet of the Guru and brought a plate of rice and dahl and served him and his companions. His every act was inspired with the spirit of service.

The banker who lived in a palatial building opposite the goldsmith's house walked in and saw the Guru lying down on the ground.

"You would have been more comfortable at my place," he remarked.

"How do you know I am less comfortable here?" answered the Guru. "On those whom He denies the goods of the world He bestows His grace. He is the Giver of the needy. I stay with His favorites so that I too may receive His gifts."

> Desire for pleasure is the disease;
> Suffering its cure.
> Peace enters the mind
> When desire for pleasure exists no more.
> When an individual ceases
> To feel he is the doer
> And knows that God is the doer,
> He abides by His will
> And enters the path of salvation.

The banker walked away with the words of the Guru ringing in his ears. Next morning he again met Nanak. "I have a favor to ask you," the Guru said to him.

The banker was flattered. "My hospitality is at your service," he answered.

"I want nothing," said the Guru, "but you are a banker and keep deposits. Will you take this needle for me. Keep it and restore it to me in the next world."

The banker laughed, and said, "You are an idiot. We can carry nothing to the other side."

"Who is an idiot, you or I? You are gathering wealth which you cannot carry, while I am seeking what can go with me."

"Come to my house," he begged, "and teach me the Way of life."

This time the Guru agreed. After they arrived, the banker said, "Tell me the way of peace. With all my possessions I have no peace. I am driven day and night on the path of misery. You are right; the whole world is in pain."

"My brother," said the Guru sweetly, "just watch the processes which bring pain. The mind is filled with desire for things; this desire acts like a barb on the mind and drives the individual towards the attainment of the object of desire. When the desired object is attained, the anxiety to protect it allows no peace. Then when the thing purchased with such pain is lost, it leaves a deeper pain behind and lastly when death comes and all is left behind, it is the culmination of agony. There is no peace in things, which are subject to change. Change itself is the source of pain. Peace can only be found in Him, the unchanging. Devotion to Him through the Sacred Name brings peace. Attachment to other things brings pain."

> Great is Your glory, O Lord all-pervading,
> Your limit no one can know or describe.
> You are in all beings, all beings are in You.
> Your incalculable power permeates the universe.
> You are the true Lord.
> Whoever adores You crosses the sea of life.
> Nanak glorifies the Lord who acts
> In the way He deems best.

The banker suddenly awoke from the ecstasy into which he had been thrown and fell at the Guru's feet.

"Save me, Great teacher," he asked. "Lift me out of the muddy waters of worldly wealth. Take me out of this morass and bless me with the gift of the Sacred Name. I ask you one more favor. Bless my wife with your presence. We had a son. He passed away and since his death my wife has been ill, unable to move from her bed. We have been devoted to each other and, though pressed on all sides, I have refused to marry again."

The Guru got up and followed the banker to his wife's room. She saw the Guru entering and in her effort to rise and receive him fell from her bed. The Guru picked her up and at the same time restored her to perfect health. The couple were astounded. They thanked the Guru over and over again.

The Guru said, "Remember all that comes into being must return to non-being. All that you give is yours, all that you keep is not yours. Make yourself a faithful servant of the Divine Will and thus earn happiness here and hereafter. Make the Sacred Name the sustenance of your lives."

.

PART III

KARTAPUR

The Guru now returned home to Kartarpur. After the morning prayers were finished, he would sit with his disciples around him and teach.

"Spiritual Master, explain to us the mystery of dreams," asked a disciple. "In a dream one sees without eyes. In a dream one hears without ears. In a dream the dead walk with the living. In a dream, not only time, but its makers, the sun and moon, do not seem to exist. In a dream future happenings are foreseen. What is it that makes dreams?"

"What you say is true," said the Guru. "Dreams bear witness to the fact that sense organs are only vehicles used by the soul on the physical plane, and that on a higher plane, the soul sees, hears, acts without its physical instruments and the barriers of time and physical death no more intervene between the living and the dead. Past, present and future are transparent in a higher state.

"In sleep," continued the Guru, "day turns into unreality and on awakening, dreams vanish and become unreal. In deep sleep both this world and the dream world cease to exist. Consciousness is aware of itself. We dream when consciousness is a witness to outer impressions. We are awake when we are aware of the existence of the world. When consciousness retires into itself beyond the bounds of waking and dreaming, nothing exists. In the foregoing states, consciousness acts within the three gunas—the phenomenal universe—but in the fourth state, which is beyond the three gunas, it becomes one with reality. All things are within the three states. In the fourth state birth and death do not exist. There the pure light dwells which is the life of the world. It is made visible through the Guru by the power of soundless sound. Life and death are subject to the three gunas. The four books of knowledge explain this. They describe three states. The fourth state, the Guru, the knower of God, alone can describe.

"Remember that all those who are born and die, as long as they are subject to the three gunas, are subject to change, pleasure and pain. It is only when consciousness reaches the fourth state, turia, that the soul is established in its own self and the individual self becomes one with the Supreme Self—the Paramatman."

"What are the three gunas?" asked another.

"Gunas are aspects of energy. Its manifestation in grosser form is Tamas; its active form is Rajas; its pure form is Satva. It is Rajas in its active form which works for action, for progress, for achievement."

Then the Guru went into a state of ecstasy and sang:

This body is like an unbaked earthen vessel;
It is made and unmade subject to suffering.
This world is an endless ocean,
It cannot be crossed without favor of the Guru.
There is no other besides You, my Beloved.
You are in all colors and forms;
He whom You favor sees You.
Like a bad mother-in-law,
The darkness of ignorance prevents union with the Beloved.
I worship the feet of the friend,
Who has favored me and removed the veil,
And I have seen my Beloved.
Having subdued the mind by meditation,
I find there is no friend other than You.
Whether You send pleasure or pain,
I shall rejoice in Your will.
In surrendering to You, hope and desire have vanished,
The domination of the gunas is at an end.
Having taken shelter with You, Your devotee,
With the favor of the Guru, has gained turia state.
Knowledge, recitation, meditation and austerities,
Are all accomplished when He, the Infinite, fills the heart.
Nanak says,
A mind that is imbued with the color of His Name,
Under the instructions of the Guru, learns to serve the Lord.

FOLLOW MY TEACHINGS NOT ME

One day while the Guru was holding his usual morning meeting, a disciple, weeping bitterly, fell at his feet and though stifled by sobs, managed to say, "I have lost my only son. I am ruined. Dear Guru, my wife and I can find no peace. We find comfort in nothing."

The Guru lifted the disciple's head and his mere touch almost cured the bereaved parent's heart-ache.

"Brother, take courage," he said. "There is none in the world who has not suffered the loss of someone dear to him. The first to depart are those under whose loving care we grow from infancy to manhood. Then one by one go those whom we love and admire. The pain has its roots in pleasure. We suffer when that which gives us joy is taken away from us. They who are wise do not attach themselves to what is passing. It is attachment to the impermanent and transitory which is the source of suffering. Everything in this world is in a state of flux. It is futile to associate intimately with what must pass. Whoever is born must die. Everyone has his turn. He, the Creator, is the only permanent being. All else comes and goes."

"Guru," said another, "what is it that lives and never dies?"

"That which is not subject to the three gunas," said the Guru, "and that which never floats and is not drowned. It is matter which partakes of the three gunas which changes. The self which gives life is changeless. Remember, he alone lives in whose heart He abides. In reality none else are alive."

The disciple bowed and asked again, "Why is the individual born and why does he die again and again?"

"The individual inspired by the will to live, persists in affirming the self, aware of his own individuality," said the Guru. "In self-assertion this world exists. Self-assertion is the bondage created by the self itself. Self-assertion is the disease, self-surrender the cure. The asserting self performs acts for the satisfaction of the self and thus builds its own character, which determines its present and its future.

"In the hope of living, the world works for its own death. The hope never dies and there is no escape from birth and death. Hope only finds fulfillment when we seek the feet of God."

A disciple who had just come, stopped for a short while and then rose to go.

"Why are you in such a hurry to depart?" inquired the Guru.

"Sir," he said, "I am taking care of a friend who is very ill and helpless. There is no one to look after him. He was feeling worse when I left him this morning, but I couldn't miss my daily sight of you."

"It is more important to follow my instructions than to come see me," said the Guru. "You have ignored my teaching by coming to me to serve yourself, instead of serving him whom God has placed in your care."

"Forgive me," said the disciple. "I have wrongly neglected my duty. I came to you to gratify myself."

"Remember," said the Guru, "that it is more important to follow what I teach than to see me. Your duty was with the patient."

"See," said the Guru, when the disciple was gone, "how self intrudes upon men of good intentions. Indeed, until the individual self melts into God-consciousness, there is no freedom from desire, from self-expression and from gratification of the self. Separation is the life-breath of the ego, and it does all it can to strengthen the will to separate. As we turn toward God, his compassion for all creation enters our hearts and as this feeling to serve our fellow-men increases, the sense of separation decreases and the individual self moves to be one with its source."

> The light of dawn breaks forth, when the ego dies.
> Then the tide of good-will for all fills the heart.
> He who sees himself in all that exists,
> He is indeed exalted, says Nanak.

The Guru continued, "Such a one becomes one with God and becomes responsive to joy and sorrow which sweep this whole creation."

Salis Rai, the jeweler, who had been listening with rapt attention, then asked, "Tell me how to find the way to happiness in this world?"

"They alone can find the way of happiness," said the Guru, "who know the Truth. Having subdued the ego, and with it the thirst for things, they are absorbed in truth."

"What happens to those," he asked, "who do not realize the Truth?"

"He who does not realize the Truth," said the Guru, "burns in the fire of desire, but he who knows his own self, becomes one with the infinite God."

"What are the characteristics of a good man?" asked the jeweler.

"A good man," said the Guru, "does not wrap himself in indifference. He returns good for evil, his heart is empty of hate and envy. He suffers when others suffer. He is happy when others are happy, while a man who is not good hates others, is indifferent to the suffering of others, and cannot bear to see anyone prosper."

"What are the characteristics of a devotee?" asked a disciple.

"A devotee," said the Guru, "is like a virgin bride, who surrenders herself to the bridegroom without any thought of self. A devotee is no more aware of his separate self in the service of the Beloved. The image of the Beloved fills his heart till all sense of separateness departs and the devotee becomes one with the object of devotion."

"Tell me, great teacher, how should a householder live?"

"Listen," said the Guru, "he who earns his living by hard labor and shares it with others, he follows the true path."

"What should be the characteristics of your disciple?"

"He who is truthful, contented and compassionate towards all, he who is free from covetousness and hate, he who is harmless, dispassionate and desireless, he who is self-controlled and has learned to discriminate between right and wrong, he who surrenders himself to the Supreme God and learns to abide by His will, such a harmonized person has entered the path of discipleship."

"MEN GAMBLE AWAY THEIR LIVES"

One day Mani Lal asked the Guru, "You say that the sacred Word has the power to change suffering into bliss, egoism into selflessness, but how is the sacred Word to possess the mind? My effort to repeat the sacred Word never reaches the heart of my being."

"It is only when we win His favor by righteous living, that we acquire the power to repeat the sacred Name."

"It sounds so easy," said Mani Lal, "when you speak, but the veil of darkness remains and refuses to be lifted."

"When we practice Truth," said the Guru, "His light illuminates the darkness of the mind and it no longer clings to this poisonous world. Living the life of a householder, a devotee, by the Guru's grace, secures salvation."

"How can I practice Truth and be worthy of the grace of the Guru?"

"It is by serving Him that we follow the path of Truth and by surrendering to Him what is His. Such service pleases the Master, and, when accepted by Him, He bestows His grace."

"It is not easy to be attached to the invisible," said Mani Lal. "It is still more difficult to know how to serve Him, when no direct service can be rendered."

"To love His creation is to serve Him," said the Guru. "Install the image of the Guru in your heart, then you will get all that you desire. The true Lord with His grace accepts such a servant and removes the fear of death from his mind."

"How should one begin to transfer the mind from worldly activities to divine activities?"

"You must begin," said the Guru, "to meditate on Truth and cultivate devotion to the True Word. The fruit of recitation and austerities is hidden in the True Word; it leads you to the door of salvation."

Another disciple said, "You once said that this mind sometimes scales the skies and at other times sinks to the lower regions. This greedy mind is never stable. It wanders in every direction."

"I am glad you mentioned that," said the Guru. "Without the control of the mind the object is never attained. A mind under the cloud of passions cannot reflect the light of Truth. It is only when clouds disperse, under the directions of the Guru, that it turns to Him again. The pure Atman has come under the sway of the gunas. It is by His grace that it is released from their sway."

"How does it pass under the sway of the gunas?" inquired the disciple.

"This is a mystery which is not easy to explain," said the Guru. "Words can only describe objects that we know and what is not known, no word can describe. Know this—that creation exists under the interaction of the three gunas and freedom is gained when their sway is over. The spirit in the state of evolution wanders in search of the objects of desire and becomes captive by the creation of its own Karma. In turning away from the objects of senses and in turning to God it finds release again and becomes one with Him."

> Body makes the paper, mind the ink,
> Good and bad deeds make the writing.
> Past actions produce our present acts,
> Wondrous are the ways of God.
> In the mad pursuit of the world,
> Why do you not remember Him?
> In forgetting Him, all virtues depart.

> Every hour makes a mesh of the net.
> In the snare of night and day
> You eagerly seek enjoyment, simpleton,
> And get more and more enmeshed in the net.

"Having entered the plane of Maya," the Guru continued, "we are lost in pursuit of illusions of Maya and find no rest. It is only by invoking His Name that we find the path of salvation.

"Men gamble away their lives," said the Guru, "for the sake of a wife, sons, houses and money. This is not the way to attain control over one's mind, which is the key of liberation.

"They who gather the wealth of the world, their minds never find rest. Pleasure and pain become their door-keepers. They can gain peace only when they turn to God. When, by Divine favor, the seeker meets the true teacher and under his directions gives up vices and acquires virtues, he then receives the gift of the Word. There is no freedom from misery without the power of the Name. They who are unrighteous cannot escape from the snare of Maya—illusion. Only by good Karma, a person becomes righteous and receives the gift of knowledge. The fickle wandering mind then becomes attached to the reality and is no more fascinated by the filth of the world. Such a person, says Nanak, chants the praises of God."

THE CREATION OF THE WORLD

A Pandit came and after attending the morning prayers asked the Guru, "Can you tell us how this world came into existence?"

"How strange," said the Guru, "that we know nothing about our own coming on this earth and we want to know how the whole creation came into being. You want to know at what time, at what epoch, at what lunar day and day of the week, in what month, in what season the world was created. If the Pandits had known this they would have recorded it in the Puranas; if the Prophet had known it, he would have recorded it in the Koran. No one knows anything about it. Only the Creator who fashioned the world knows it." Then the Guru closed his eyes and uttered the following hymn:

For an unlimited period there was darkness. There was neither heaven nor earth, there was only the boundless Word. There was neither sun nor moon, neither day nor light. He alone was in a state of Samadhi. There were no species nor speech, neither air nor water. No creation nor its dissolution, nor birth nor death. Neither there were divisions of the earth, nor the seven regions; neither were there oceans nor rivers, nor was there water flowing.

A WISE BOY

The Guru started a regular devotional service for his disciples at Kartarpur. They rose before dawn, had their bath, and recited Jap-ji followed by the singing of hymns. The day was started with the heart full of God. In the evening Rahras was recited, followed by the singing of Arti, and at bedtime the Sohilla was sung. Morning, noon and night the disciples of the Guru were instructed to live in the light of true teachings.

There was a boy of about seven years of age who regularly attended the early morning service and never missed a congregational prayer.

"My son," the Guru asked him one day, "what brings you here? At your age boys sleep till late in the morning and play all day."

The boy bowed to the Guru with folded hands and touched his feet. "It is you who call me here," he said. "One day my mother asked me to light a fire. I found that little sticks caught the fire before the thick ones were ignited, so I thought any day my turn might come and I decided to prepare myself."

"You speak like an old man and you are indeed wise. I'll call you Bhai Buddha. You are right, life is like a flowing stream that appears and disappears in hills and valleys. It is well to be prepared and to fill the mind with one color only. That is His color."

One of the audience then rose and asked, "If we act under His command, have we no free will of our own? Without it how can we seek salvation?"

"Have I not already said that God's Name has the power of liberation and of releasing the seeker from the bondage of acts which bind. But it is again by His grace that this secret is discovered. Our acts are determined as long as I-AM-NESS rules, but when we free ourselves from I-AM-NESS we exercise free will."

The boy devotee from that day was known as Bhai Buddha and was much respected by the Guru himself and his successors. He was held in such esteem that he was given the privilege of conferring Guruship on five successors of Guru Nanak.

GURMUKH—MANMUKH

"Sir, you always say that a Gurmukh—a God conscious man—is exalted and a Manmukh—an egocentric man—remains bankrupt. Teach us how to distinguish between the two," asked a disciple.

"He is holy, he is righteous, he is a Gurmukh who is sympathetic and happy in the happiness of others."

"How are they known, Guru," asked another.

"By their actions," said the Guru. "A Gurmukh is pleased at hearing the praises of others. He serves the poor and the needy. He shows honor and respect to the virtuous and the learned and all those who follow the way. He avoids subjects of discussions which give rise to quarrels. He serves those who are superior to him in intelligence or devotion. He uses his power, not arrogantly in trampling the rights of others, but in protecting them. His pure intentions find expression in daily actions, such as faithfulness to his wife, respect for all other women, and avoidance of evil company. Seeking the society of holy men, as a result of good living, the craving for God's Name grows in intensity and he cannot find rest without His Name."

Two students asked, "How can one become a Gurmukh?"

The Guru said, "By avoiding Manmukh Karma—evil acts."

"What is Manmukh Karma?" they asked.

"Know him to be a Manmukh who is envious of everyone and who regards all men as his enemies and hates them; who desires that worldly wealth and all happiness should desert others and come to him.

"He who follows the Guru's instructions is a Gurmukh, and who turns away his face from them and follows the impulses of his own mind is a Manmukh. A Manmukh is relentless and proud. He laughs at persons inferior to him, treats them with contempt, and glories in his own intelligence. A Manmukh is addicted to slander. If anyone praises another who is superior to him, a Manmukh cannot endure it and exclaims, 'Oh, I know him well; he is not what he appears to be!' He obstinately follows the impulses of his selfish mind. All his actions express envy, pride, slander and obstinacy. He who is conceited, who is envious, cannot follow the path of the Guru. They who turn to the Guru drop these tendencies as trees drop their leaves in autumn and wear their new garments in spring."

 ## SHADOWS

One morning, just at sunrise, the Guru walked to the river Ravi which flowed close by. Some of his disciples followed him. They were walking with the sun behind them.

One of the disciples moved forward, bowed and asked the Guru, "How is it that we cannot dispel the illusions of Maya?"

"Just look at the shadows," said the Guru. "You can travel miles and miles and your shadows will precede you so long as the sun is at your back. Now turn your faces towards the sun; where are the shadows?"

"They have disappeared," they said. "They are left behind."

"Learn this," said the Guru, "as long as our faces are turned away from God, the shadows of Maya hold us, but as soon as you turn your faces toward God, the shadows disappear."

"What prevents our turning toward God," they asked.

"A man is born because in him there is desire to become. Driven by desire, he lives and enjoys the fruits of the earth. At death he carries the seed which his actions fed, and is bound by it. He reaps in suffering, the fruit of his wrong doings. It is only when he follows the right path as instructed by the Guru that he secures his release by the power of the sacred Name."

"It is not easy to follow the right path," said several disciples. "How should one prepare for the journey's end?"

"Seek the company of men in whose mind God dwells. Listen to what they say, sing the praises of God and in doing so, surrender your will to the Divine Will. Under such a discipline, the wandering mind will cease to pursue sense-objects. It will find satisfaction in dwelling on God and turn from the unreal to the real."

"You say, sir, that we should perform the duties of the household. How can these be performed without concentrating the mind on their performance?"

"I can explain to you but you will not understand until your mind turns toward God. When that happens, your heart will be with the Beloved, and your hands will perform the acts. The mind that is God-filled is only conscious of Him and unconscious of all else. All acts are then performed under the light of Divine Command."

"How should a devotee live?" asked a disciple.

"Look at the river over there, flowing without pause under the

117

command of the law of nature. Let your life flow as the river under Divine Command, submit yourself to the Divine Will as an anvil submits to the hammering of the blacksmith, always placing its head before the hammer. Thus place your body and mind at the service of the Lord and serve Him through pain and suffering. Thus we gain the key to the closed door."

"Why is it that Sat Nam, the True Name, precedes all hymns?" asked a disciple.

"Some invoke Durga, some Shiva, some Ganesh and some other gods, but the true disciple worships only one God whose Name is true. His Name is above all that exists in all the worlds. Therefore, we seek his protection by invoking His Name at the beginning of all hymns."

One day a disciple approached the Guru with folded hands. "Guru, Hindus and Muslims follow laws given by their law-givers and the prophets. What law must we follow?"

"The law of Truth," said the Guru. "Falsehood fades away, but the Truth prevails."

"How is it that every action arouses a feeling of uncertainty and consequently fear?"

"All actions are performed in a threefold manner: first desire arises in the mind, secondly it finds expression in speech and thirdly it impels the organs of action to act. All actions are performed to meet the demands of desire, and consequently are shadowed by anxiety and fear, lest failure may haunt the effort instead of success. The fear of losing what has been acquired fills the mind with unceasing anxiety."

THE DAY DRAWS NEAR

The successor to Makhdoom, Pir Bhah-ud-Din had met the Guru in Multan. Now that he felt that his journey on earth was drawing to a close, he came to see the Guru. The Guru welcomed him. He said, "My boat is now loaded and ready to take to the unknown seas. Can you help me to lighten the load?"

"My friend," said the Guru, "we carry the sack which we have carefully filled, but the grace of His mercy can lighten the load of those who empty their heart of self and stand at His door for forgiveness."

The Pir sat silent, lost in deep meditation.

"I also feel," said the Guru, "that I have fulfilled my mission and must return home. I feel happy that the day is drawing near."

In a village lived Khadur Lehna, a great devotee of the goddess of flame. He visited her temple twice a year, walking full of devotion to offer his humble savings at her feet. He often met a man called Jodha, who also lived in the same village and heard from Jodha the hymns of Guru Nanak. Lehna was much impressed by what Jodha told him and begged him to take him to the Guru. Jodha readily agreed and they both came together to Kartarpur and joined the crowd that had gathered around the Guru. They attended the morning prayer, and listened to the praises of God sung by the choir. For a few days Lehna quietly listened to the sermons delivered by the Guru. Lehna was deeply stirred by the prayers sung and the inner chords of his heart were touched. He immediately discarded the thread he wore round his neck as a sign of belonging to the cult of the goddess, and he came forward and fell at the feet fo the Guru.

"Accept me, great teacher," he pleaded.

The Guru lifted him with his own hands, and said, "I have been waiting for your coming. What is your name?"

"My name is Lehna, which means the receiver."

The Master smiled and said, "You are indeed a receiver. You must take what I owe you."

The Guru embraced Lehna, and, in that embrace, endowed him with light.

"You have now become one with me, and from now on you will be known as Angad—one with me in body and soul."

One day a Yogi who practiced breath control came to the Guru and asked, "Great teacher, tell me how it is that in spite of performing prolonged Pranayamas, my mind can never gain tranquility. It wanders even in the process of my meditation and afterwards entirely without control."

"The answer is simple," said the Guru. "You wish to control the mind by control of breath, which is a physical process, and the mind is superphysical and therefore it is beyond the control of mere physical action. Till mind itself is washed clean, it can never be tranquil. When mind becomes tranquil, breathing is automatically stopped."

"They say," said the Yogi, "that there are nadis—hidden streams of power—within this body, and that by the inhalation and exhalation of breath, these can be stirred. And the control of breath subdues the usual activities of the mind, as it becomes motionless with the stopping of breath. In Hatha Yoga the right nostril, Pingala, is the vehicle of the sun, the left side, Ida, that of the moon. The breath inhaled through the right nostril partakes of the sun, is retained in Sushumna — the central stream which is called Brahmnadi, and is exhaled through Ida. The retaining of breath in Sushumna awakens the hidden powers of Kundalini."

"My dear friend," said the Guru, "you are well-versed in the system of Hatha Yoga. You have no doubt discovered through practice that these outer restraints cannot awaken the soul and secure salvation without the protection and guidance of the Holy Name. You may acquire superphysical powers, but they perish with the body. It is not by drawing on the sun or the moon, but by drawing up the sun—that is, by overcoming the energy from which actions spring, and by nourishing the moon, the spirit of mellow tranquility, that the vagrant mind, which wanders like the wind and is restless like a fish, is brought under control. By controlling the motive power, consciousness can no longer fly and dart in all directions but abides in the inner temple, protected by ramparts of virtue.

"WORDS ARE USELESS"

One day the disciples of Sheik Behram, a devotee of the Guru, came to see him. They had been asking the Sheik many questions so he told them to go to Guru Nanak who would answer them.

"Tell us something of the Beloved," asked the leader of the party.

"Listen," said the Guru:

> The Beloved himself is the enjoyer,
> Himself the essence of the enjoyment,
> Himself appears in bridal robes,
> Himself the bridegroom of the bridal bed.
> My Lord and Master is resplendent
> In His glory.
> He pervades all things.
> He Himself is the flowing water,
> Himself the fisherman,
> Himself the net,
> Himself the fisherman's hook,
> Himself the fish, Himself the hidden ruby.
> O my friends, in an infinite variety of colors
> Appears my Beloved.
> He meets His devotee daily,
> May he have compassion on us.

120

Praise Him, He is the lake,
He is the swan, He is the lotus in bud.
Himself the lotus in bloom,
Its witness and its enjoyer.

Angad bowed and asked, "My Guru, why are some accepted and some not accepted?"

"Close your eyes and look within," said the Guru. "Words are useless; experience affords true revelation."

Angad obeyed and when he opened his eyes he was full of gladness.

The leader of the Sufis asked, "What has made you so happy?"

"I cannot tell," said Angad. "He is all in all."

"Listen," said the Guru, "He alone who tastes this delicacy knows its taste. He cannot tell just as a dumb man cannot describe the taste of the sweets he enjoys. What can one say about Him, who cannot be described? All that is given to us is to abide by His will and thus become harmonized."

"Tell us more," asked another. "How can we appear with shining faces before Him?"

"He appears with a shining face whose self dies while living, who destroys the ego, who breaks his bonds and whose thirst for things is quenched. The sacred Word dwells in all beings, but only rare true seekers discover it."

"How can we discover it," asked several voices.

"Five evils are embedded in the innermost recesses of the mind. These give it no rest and the mind wanders ceaselessly."

"How do they affect the mind?" asked another.

"These five enemies generate thirst for things. Desire burns like a fire and, like thirst or hunger, is never wholly satisfied."

"How can its fire be quenched?"

"The fire of desire can only be extinguished by the sacred Word. First we must begin a struggle with the mind, subdue these five enemies, then the desire vanishes and the mirror of the mind is ready to reflect His light. The one thing we need to control is the mind and to prevent its wandering."

"But this mind eludes control," said the questioner.

"Yes," said the Guru. "But till the mind is subdued, light does not shine in it. With the conquering of the mind the whole universe is conquered."

The Guru continued, "A novice must begin by exercising control over the mind by continuous watchfulness over thoughts. When these are brought under control, there will arise the power of discrimination between the good and the bad, the changing and unchanging, the real and unreal. It is only thus that true knowledge is gained and not by cleverness of the mind."

The immortal bird that can discriminate
Between milk and water, good and bad,
Finds joy at the lake of knowledge,
Which is brimful with rare pearls
On which the immortal bird feeds.
The heron and the wise crow,
They never discover this lake,
For their food is not in it.
What they need is quite different.
They who work for Truth attain Truth;
They who work for untruth remain in untruth.
They who receive His commands from above
Meet the Sat Guru.

"IF YOU ARE STRONG HELP THE WEAK"

A famous religious philosopher came to the Guru and discoursed on salvation by knowledge with a great display of learning. The Guru heard him patiently and then asked him, "What do you know of Brahma?"

"I know all that the Vedas and Shastras teach about him," he answered.

"If salvation can be attained by knowledge, you must surely have attained it."

The philosopher hesitated; he could not honestly say that his knowledge had given him the key to realization.

The Guru said, "Words are but symbols. Reality itself must be realized to obtain salvation."

"I know all is Brahma," said the philosopher, "but I cannot rid myself of the limitations of my own self."

"This feeling of separation must vanish," said the Guru, "before you can claim knowledge of Him, who is beyond comprehension. All humanity is conscious of its own existence. Only a few can abolish the barriers which I-AM-NESS raises and become one with him."

When I am aware of my own self,
Then I am not aware of Him.
When I realize Him,
Then I cease to be.
Now, Philosopher, solve that riddle.
The secret hidden beyond the reach of mind,
The Unknowable, dwells in the heart.
He is not discovered without the instruction of the Guru.
It is only when the true teacher is met,

122

That we realize He dwells within.
When Self disappears, fear disappears,
And with it the pain of birth and death.

"What kind of actions should we perform?" the philosopher asked. "And what kind of actions should we avoid?"

"Actions which are performed to gratify the self, actions which harm others, actions which are hypocritical are evil and should be avoided. Actions which are performed without any personal motive, actions which help others are good. If you are strong, help the weak.

"Remember, this body is the dwelling place of God. Nothing should be done which is not pleasing to God who is within you. The records of all acts are read out in the presence of the Lord of Justice. According to their deeds, some draw near and others are driven away to an even greater distance."

"As long as life is in the body, it must perform action. All actions create Karma which governs the present," the philosopher said. "Can we sterilize the seed of Karma by any means?"

"If we surrender ourselves to God and act as the instruments of His will, we sow no seed of action. The sacrificial fire of devotion consumes the seed of all our actions."

"How can one follow the Divine Will?" asked another. "God gives no direct commands."

"This creation is of God, and when we serve His creation, we serve Him and obey His commands. When we use our body for the service of others we create no personal Karma, but fulfill the Divine purpose, and if every breath of ours is charged with the Sacred Name, all our acts are then performed in the Divine presence."

A TRUE DISCIPLE—A SIKH

One day the Guru was sitting on the bank of the river when a disciple fell into the water. The Guru himself got him out and saved him from being drowned. When the disciple regained consciousness he fell at the Guru's feet.

The Guru asked him, "Tell me, when you went under water, what was uppermost in your mind?"

The disciple replied, "I had lost all consciousness and desired only one thing—breath."

The Guru addressing all those present said, "When a man becomes unconscious of everything else and desires God with all his power, then he attains Bhakti—devotion." The Guru continued, "Taste in the fish, sound in the snake, smell in the bee, passion for light in the moth, and pleasure of touch in the elephant, all of which are desires for the object of the senses, are the causes of their destruction. Brothers, we human beings have not one but five senses to mislead us. In the pursuit of sense-objects we perish. Therefore, have one and one Object alone for all the five senses. Desire only one Object, and that Object will be obtained. Forget yourself entirely in desiring that Object. By desiring that, all desires are satisfied.

"Most people profess to love others, but they only love themselves; a few love those who love them, but a true disciple of the Guru—a Sikh—must love all, even those who hate him.

"The whole world works for gain, only a few work because it is their duty to work. Only a rare one works without any desire for a return. But a follower of the Guru—a Sikh— must serve friends and foes alike, knowing that it is only thus he can serve God.

"Everyone lives for the sake of the self. Some share what they gain with others; a rare one finds enjoyment in giving to others, a true devotee of the Guru—a Sikh—must live entirely for others.

"People endeavor to promote their interest by aggressiveness. Some people work for personal ends without any aggressiveness. A rare one works for all humanity. A devotee of the Guru—a Sikh— rejoices in carrying out the will of God.

"Most people want their own names to be exalted. A few want their friends to be exalted. There are a few who desire neither name nor fame. A student of the Guru—a Sikh—exalts the Name of God, without any sense of self."

The Guru began to prepare himself for his departure. He had endowed Angad with his own spirit, but he wanted to prove to his disciples that Angad was worthy to succeed him. He tested him in many ways, and proved his faith in himself and his contact with the Divine.

Then one day in an open meeting he placed Angad on his own seat and bowed to him in acknowledgment. The Guru then left his residence and sat under a withered tree which burst into green foliage on his presence.

The news that the Guru had decided to leave the world spread far and wide, and disciples flocked round him from all directions. The Guru sat serene and undisturbed and spoke to the crowd, telling them that his mission had been fulfilled and they would make him happy if they rejoiced with him on his return Home.

> Hail to the Creator, the true King, who allotted to the
> world its various duties.
> When the measure is full, the duration of life is at an
> end, the soul is led away.
> When the destined hour arrives, the soul is led away and
> all one's relations weep.
> The body and soul are separated, O my mother, when
> one's days are at an end.
> You have obtained what was allotted you, and reaped the
> fruit of your former acts.
> Hail to the Creator, the true King, who allotted the world
> its various duties.
> Remember the Lord, O my brothers. All must depart.
> The affairs of this world are transitory. After a short time
> here, we must proceed onward.
> Why should we be proud? We must proceed onward like
> a gust.
> Repeat the Name of Him by whose worship you shall
> obtain happiness in His Court.
> In the next world, you can in no way enforce your
> authority.
> Everyone shall fare according to his acts.
> Remember the Lord, my brothers. Everyone must depart.
> That which pleases the Omnipotent shall come to pass.
> This world is an illusion.
> The true Creator pervades sea and land, the nether regions
> and the firmament.
> His limit cannot be found. The true Creator is invisible,
> unequalled.

Profitable is their advent into this world, who have
meditated with their whole hearts upon Him.
The adorner, by His order, demolishes and again
constructs.
That which pleases the Omnipotent shall come to pass.
This world is an illusion.
Says Nanak, O father, they shall be considered to have
wept who weep through love.
If men weep for the sake of worldly things, all their
weeping, O father, shall be in vain.
All their weeping shall be in vain. The world is not
mindful of God and weeps for greed.
They distinguish not good from evil, and thus lose their
human lives.
False are they who practice pride. All who come into this
world must depart.
Says Nanak, men shall be considered to have wept, O
father, if they weep through love.

EPILOGUE

Guru Nanak drew a white sheet over himself and left this world. Flowers dropped from the heavens. Celestial music was heard. Immediately a dispute arose between Hindus and Muslims. The Hindus wanted to cremate him, the Muslims bury him. When they lifted the sheet, the Guru's body wasn't there. The sheet was cut into two pieces. One piece was taken by the Hindus, the other by the Muslims. A tomb and shrine were erected by the side of the River Ravi. Later these were washed away by the river.

A LIBERATED MAN
by Yogi Bhajan

What is a liberated man? And what is the reason we suffer in the hands of time?

Man has two sides. One is a carefree side. The other is a careless side. When man lives in his carefree side, he is guided by his Divine faculty. When he lives in his careless side he is guided by his animal force. It is not the carelessness of breaking a glass or accidentally throwing away something you meant to keep. Materially we are considered careless when we are unable to discharge our material responsibilities, but in reality, we are truly careless when we lose our Divine personality — when that "something" which is very precious, beyond value, is lost just for passion.

Emotion and passion are the two buyers of our Spiritual personality. If you analyze this thought you will realize that such a bargain is too costly. For what are we trading our Spiritual Self?

This world of ours is a transitory phase of life. It is not permanent, but we always associate ourselves with it as if we belong to it and it belongs to us. Subconsciously, behind every action is the desire to be recognized. But if you classify your desire for recognition and the way you try to be recognized, you will find that you want recognition without maturity. You want to be recognized as a mature being, but you have not developed the mature attitude of a carefree being.

The only carefree being is that person who is free from negativity. He is liberated. It is a Cosmic Law that such a person is never short of anything. A carefree man doesn't know any misery. He may be humble, but that doesn't mean he is miserable. Ever wise, he sails through time undisturbed. He does not need any correction at the hands of time. His smooth behavior and calmness of personality are the signs that he is a liberated being. In a nutshell, he is the happiest person ever on the earth.

This does not mean that you should be barred from having worldly goods. Matter is media. It cannot be created and it cannot be destroyed. Similarly, emotion and involvement in desire are also media, but their satisfaction is temporary, not everlasting. If you understand how the addiction to liquor begins, you will understand this theory of involvement. This is how it works. A man who does not drink comes under pressure and doesn't know what to do. He goes to the house of a friend for consolation, for man is a social animal, and by having someone participate in his grief, he feels relieved. The friend offers whiskey for a soothing effect and the man is persuaded to take a drink. The alcohol goes into the body and does its chemical action. It soothes the nerves, and energizes the energy centers so that the man's attitude relaxes and becomes flexible. It is only a temporary relief, but the memory of the first taste sticks in his mind. He can never ever regain the smoothness of that first taste of liquor, but for the lust of that taste and in order to recapture that experience, people become habitual drinkers — alcoholics. They believe that the best way to escape from the pressures of life is to continue drinking and thus drinking becomes a need of the body.

Similarly, whenever you involve yourself in any mode of life, you are going into a channel where you will go on and on and on, and you can never come back to the point from which you originally started. When we forget our original basis of action and become involved, we become a slave.

It has been seen in our entire concept of life, that we are 15% slaves to routine, to habit. Man must have certain habits without which his life cannot go on. But he can attain liberation by changing the character of these minimum required habits. There are two kinds of habits: Promoting habits and demoting habits. Demoting habits make you unhappy physically, mentally and spiritually. Promoting habits make you happy physically, mentally and spiritually. In your life, if you have all the habits which are promoting habits, you will end up as a Liberated, Divine person. If you have demoting habits, you will always end up as a physical wreck, mentally insane and/or spiritually defunct.

Habit is a must of your personality and mind. For that period when you are acting under a demoting habit, you are totally in the hands of Satan or the negative personality. It is also a fact that if you get into any one negative habit, you will automatically attract its four sister habits, for they love to stay together. These five demoting habits of behavior and attitude are: greed, anger, lust, attachment and negative ego. When one sister enters the house, she calls the others to join. Each habit is supported on two tripods — 1) Physical, Mental and Spiritual, and 2) Past, Present and Future.

There are two guiding instincts in man. He is either improving his future or blocking his future improvement. If you are conscious of this, and have an honest and sincere urge to improve your future, you will always have promoting habits. *Oh man, if you are to care not even for God, at least care for the future.* When you care enough for your future to have promoting habits, you will become a liberated person.

A liberated person is always a happy person. He does not lack in any material comfort. He does not know any power on earth which can insult him. He lives in grace in this world and when he leaves the body he is respected for generations to follow. Everyone can be like that. Yesterday's greatest sinner can be a Saint this minute. The only thing required is a decision. "Am I to guard my

130

future and choose to be a liberated person, or am I to block my future and go by the material-physical aspect of the world?" For any person who blocks his future, it is a guaranteed fact he suffers in the future. Any person who takes advantage of the "now" — causes someone else's loss — blocks his future. Anyone who takes advantage of the "now" invites trouble from Mr. Future.

Maintain a positive attitude with promoting habits for 40 days, and you can change your destiny. This psychological concept of Human behavior is a pattern which can guide you to that goal which is described in our scriptures as Paradise.

In the self one has to sow the seed of Divine vibrations and with the power of these vibrations one has to dwell in the Ultimate which is a Truth, a reality and an ever living primal force. This primal force has been named God by Christians; Paramatman by Hindus; Allah by Muslims. Some name has been given it by all — but the Universal Consciousness or this Universal Spirit has one name, that is Truth, so we call it Sat and we remember it as Sat Nam. Sat, in the language of Gods, Sanskrit, means Truth; Nam means Name. So without dispute we can say that Universal Consciousness, that Universal Spirit, that creative force in us, has a universal name and that is Sat Nam. All those who want to liberate themselves and seek to dwell in the Ultimate must cleanse their physical selves and direct their mental beings towards the Sat Nam, the being of beings. One who dwells on the vibrations of this Holy Nam — Sat Nam — in the prime hours of the day before dawn when the channels for vibrations are very clean and clear will realize the concept of a liberated man through the grace of this Bij Mantra which awakens the goddess of awareness in a being. He then lives as a liberated man on the planet Earth.

ੴ ਸਤਿਨਾਮ ਸ੍ਰੀ ਵਾਹਿਗੁਰੂ